Thank you for your interest in and purchase of this new book *Unmasking ISIS* by Terry Law and James Gilbert.

We hope you will find the book both informational and inspirational as you learn the real story behind ISIS and their terrorist activities throughout the world.

Hopefully with the material presented and recommendations made we can help you be better prepared to respond to what you see and hear each day concerning the great challenge of terrorism worldwide.

For more information about our global mission and work visit us at www.worldcompassion.tv

Jason Law	Terry Law
President	Founder
	Chairman of the Board

UNMASKING ISIS

DEFEATING THE TERRORISTS
WHO WANT TO DESTROY THE WORLD

UNMASKING ISIS

TERRY LAW & JAMES GILBERT

UNMASKING ISIS

Defeating the Terrorists Who Want To Destroy the World

Copyright © 2016 by Terry Law

Published by Terry Law: Storm Chaser LLC
www.stormchaser.org

Library of Congress Cataloging-in-Publication Data
Applied for

ISBN: 978-1-53074-585-2

Printed in the United States of America

Design: Peter Gloege | LOOK Design Studio

Editorial development and creative design support by Ascent:
www.itsyourlifebethere.com

Follow Terry Law:
TerryLawSC @TerryLawSC StormChaser.org

Follow James Gilbert:
JamesGilbertWrites @JamesGatLarge

To the martyrs, whose blood cries out in heaven,

And to their widowed and orphaned,

May your cries be heard throughout the earth

CONTENTS

PROLOGUE 9

1 THE REASON FOR TERROR 17

2 WARRIORS OF THE END OF DAYS 29

3 WHY DO THEY HATE US? 43

4 THE LURE OF THE CALIPHATE 51

5 SEDUCING CALIPHETTES 63

6 DID WE CAUSE ISIS? 77

7 BLOOD MONEY 91

8 IS THIS WORLD WAR III? 101

9 FROM DARKNESS TO DAWN 113

10 NINE STEPS AMERICA'S LEADERS CAN TAKE NOW 129

11 NINE STEPS YOU CAN TAKE NOW 143

EPILOGUE 155

NOTES 165

ACKNOWLEDGMENTS 173

ABOUT THE AUTHORS 175

PROLOGUE

THE GASP HEARD ROUND THE WORLD

The headlines on June 10, 2014 were astounding enough: 800 Islamic State terrorists—from the same group that U.S. President Barack Obama only months earlier had called "the jayvee squad"—had routed 30,000 American-trained Iraqi troops and seized Mosul, the second largest city in Iraq. Then, within days, the civilized world's astonishment turned to horror, as one-by-one, reports of unimaginable atrocities began trickling across, then flooding, the newswires.

"I'm almost in tears because I've just had somebody in my room whose little child was cut in half," grieved the Anglican Vicar of Baghdad, Andrew White, in early August. "I baptized his child in my church in Baghdad. This little boy, they named him after me—he was called Andrew."[1] Four months later, the same Canon White told of four young boys who had been beheaded for refusing to deny Jesus and follow Muhammad. "They chopped all their heads off," he said. "How do you respond to that? You just cry."[2]

Day after day, for weeks and then months, the stories kept coming, each one more harrowing than the last. Husbands slaughtered and their wives and daughters sold as sex slaves on the open market, complete with "sales" designed to attract new recruits. Accused thieves crucified in midtown Mosul and homosexuals thrown from the tops of buildings to their deaths. A Jordanian pilot caged, doused with gasoline and set on fire. 74 children buried alive, crucified or shot in the head for the "crime" of not fasting during Ramadan. Severed heads mounted on poles in town squares as warnings to anyone reluctant to convert to ISIS' 7th-Century brand of Islam.

And all of it on video—ISIS always makes sure of that.

As time ticks by and the gruesomeness grows, Canon White's question rings louder than ever: How do you respond to such savagery?

You. Personally.

If you're the average American, you probably tried at first to identify with the victims and comprehend the killers, but quickly realized that neither was possible. Then, being a person of conscience, you might have said a prayer, or sent an email to your Congressman, or even tried to find a trustworthy charity attempting to help those fortunate enough to escape. More than likely, however, at some point you did the one thing that nearly all Americans do when they simply cannot stomach any more bad news: You changed the channel.

That's nothing to be guilt-ridden about. Even starting this book was a gut-wrenching chore for the authors, who took many sanity-saving breaks during our research. More than once, we uttered "thank God for ESPN," or headed out for an early lunch, or stared at an uncooperative page until the weariness of our eyes gave in to that of our souls.

But eventually we knew we had to get this job done and provide you with some very important information. And here's the first of it:

ISIS is here, in America, and we can't just change the channel anymore.

No longer can left-wing ideologues theorize that the terrorists are disaffected youth without jobs, or conservative isolationists claim "it's not our war." Neither can politically-disengaged religious leaders give cursory acknowledgment to the ongoing slaughter as some distant fulfillment of Bible prophecy that piques our curiosity without interrupting our lives.

ISIS is here. And even if they are somehow obliterated and their "caliphate" dismantled, it is inevitable that the Hydra of militant Islam will keep growing new heads who vow to sever ours, who live to bring death, and whose sole purpose in the world is to end it—not just Israel or America, but the whole world.

Which brings us back to Canon White's overarching question: How do we—all of us—respond to such savagery?

The answer lies in addressing a series of questions. And they need to be the *right* ones, lest we dig ourselves into an even deeper hole with unprofitable ones, such as:

» Is the U.S. Government riddled with Muslim sympathizers?

» Are widespread U.S. military exercises part of a plot to suspend the Constitution?

» Are all Muslims closet jihadists?

» Is everything that's happening in the Middle East a sign of the End Times?

Such questions are unhelpful simply because they invite reaction rather than action. Conspiracy theory inevitably results in a circle-the-wagons mentality, while speculating about how ISIS-related events fulfill Bible prophecy leads millions of Christians to do nothing more than look upward and wait.

We live in a time when asking what Washington is going to do about this or that issue has become almost reflexive. Compounding our inaction is the fact that politicians, regulators and bureaucrats now ask themselves the same question, because they too have come to assume that it is not only their responsibility but their *right* to manage our lives. And for a host of reasons, that philosophy isn't working.

Yes, the President of the United States, as Commander-in-Chief, is ultimately responsible to provide for the common defense, and yes, Congress and the Judiciary have a role to play, as well. But simply asking "What is the Government going to do about ISIS?" isn't nearly enough. Not anymore. Just ask the workers at Vaughn Foods in Oklahoma City, where in September 2014 a recently-fired, lone-wolf jihadist stormed the company offices and beheaded a 54-year-old grandmother who worked there. Or the families of the 14 county employees killed by an ISIS-radicalized co-worker in San Bernardino, California, in December 2015. Or the widows and widowers of Fort Hood, Texas.

ISIS is here.

Their recruits don't need membership cards to join. They just need to kill somebody in Oklahoma, California, or Texas—or where you live—in the name of Allah.

That's why we can no longer afford to change the channel. It's time to take action—action that begins by asking the *right* kinds of questions, like:

- » What worldview drives ISIS, particularly their beliefs about an end-time apocalypse?
- » How did they grow so strong and so wealthy so quickly? What about the money trail?
- » Does ISIS pervert Islam? Is their brand the real thing, or is it really a religion of peace?
- » How does the promise of a *caliphate* (a borderless, world-wide Islamic kingdom) help attract and radicalize ISIS' new recruits?

» Why do Islamists hate America in particular? Are there historical roots for their hatred?

» How does ISIS differ from al Qaeda, Hamas, Boko Haram and all the other bad players?

» Could the Sunni/Shi'a divide lead to all-out war in the Middle East?

» Does America's new "ally" Iran pose a greater long term threat than ISIS?

These are just some of the questions that we'll answer in the following chapters. And we'll keep those answers simple, short and practical, while drawing on the knowledge we have each gained from decades working not only in the Muslim world, but also several other strife-filled regions around the globe.

Dr. Terry Law has worked extensively in Afghanistan, Iraq and Iran since 2002, distributing humanitarian aid through his Christian relief agency, World Compassion, headquartered in Tulsa, Oklahoma. In 2005, Terry successfully petitioned the Iraqi interim government to include a religious freedom clause in their new constitution, and in 2007 negotiated with the Sunni sheiks of Iraq's Anbar province to join the U.S.-led military "surge," a move that helped bring an end to that phase of the region's war. In earlier decades, he conducted equally extensive missions to the Soviet Union, Poland, China and other closed nations.

Dr. Law's biography, *Storm Chaser: The Terry Law Story,*[3] was written by coauthor James Gilbert and published in early 2015. James also brings a near-lifetime of experience to the present work. Since 1969, his career as an author, mission statesman and public speaker has taken him into more than 60 nations, with special emphasis on the communist world.

As a narrative, *Storm Chaser* ends on April 8, 2013, with Terry Law celebrating his jubilee birthday at the international airport in Athens, Greece, where he welcomed to freedom an Iraqi Christian code-named Jamal, whose supposedly impossible release from prison Terry had secured days earlier. Purposely hidden from western media, Jamal's pardon for the "crime" of converting Muslims to Christianity was a historic first in Iraq, if not in the 1,400-year history of Islam. After his release, Jamal, with his wife and children, had stayed in hiding while awaiting the family's flight to Athens.

Yet even as Terry and the jubilant family celebrated Jamal's freedom around an upstairs table in a small Athens restaurant later that evening, another virtually unnoticed but nonetheless historic "storm" was beginning to brew some 800 miles to the east. That night, behind heavily guarded doors in Raqqa, Syria, one Abu Bakr al-Baghdadi, the *de facto* leader of a band of terrorists known as al Qaeda in Iraq, raised a black flag and proclaimed a new nation: the "Islamic State of Iraq and al Sham."

At that moment, the world changed, although most people didn't notice until the next year, when ISIS began churning out slickly produced but nauseating propaganda videos of what might be best described as serial carnage, captured the Iraqi cities of Mosul and Tikrit, and announced the restoration of the caliphate. Since then, little has been done to effectively halt the bloodletting, largely because the U.S. and other Western powers insist upon seeing ISIS in non-religious political terms, rather than admit that Baghdadi and his brigade of vampires are motivated by a religion that *requires* political expression. Such official obstinacy leaves the public frightened, confused and asking questions like those posed above.

It was in this atmosphere that the authors became aware of the need for a thorough but concise overview of ISIS, *aka* ISIL (Islamic

State of Iraq and the Levant), *aka* DAESH (an Arabic acronym that ISIS considers insulting). To be sure, several good, in-depth articles and books about the group were already in print, but most were political and cultural analyses, with none meeting the popular need for a shorter, yet well-rounded explanation of who these terrorists are, why they want to kill us and how to defeat them.

Six weeks later we were in Kurdistan, northern Iraq, interviewing Interior Minister Karim Sinjari, Kurdish General Aziz Waisi, commander of the *Peshmerga*, the only army successfully fighting ISIS, and the Syriac Orthodox Archbishop of Mosul, as well as refugee families from the Nineveh Plain who in the summer of 2014 lost their homes and all they possessed as they fled ISIS for their lives. As a result of that journey, and nearly three dozen previous missions to the region, we are able to bring to this brief work a combination of journalistic insight, vast regional experience and the priceless currency of local trust.

We have worked to keep this book the primer that heretofore has been missing from today's ISIS compendium. Nonetheless, it should be seen as *a tool to help you in your own research*, rather than as a substitute for it. Taking personal responsibility is especially important during these critical days. For one thing, as we write, America is in the throes of a presidential campaign, and candidates of every stripe are trolling for votes. As is always the case that means speaking in the loftiest of tones and making the kinds of promises that so often are either forsaken after winning the prize, or simply flattened beneath the weight of the office.

"I'll strike ISIS with massive force once and for all," vows the Hawk.

"Another war won't accomplish anything and I won't send troops," counters the Dove.

Meanwhile, *ISIS is here*, and regardless of which candidate actually has the best ideas, you need:

» to be informed and settled in your own views

» to know how to pressure authorities at every level to implement policies that make sense to you

» to take practical action to make your town, your home and your family as safe and secure as possible

Our goal is to help you ask the important questions, get clear answers, and take prudent action, not only as a responsible citizen, but also as the average Joe who wants to protect his family, or the single Jill who's honestly worried that *her* subway train might be next on some bomber's list. That's why this book is titled *Unmasking ISIS: Defeating the Terrorists Who Want to Destroy the World.*

1

THE REASON FOR TERROR

"Let there be no compulsion in religion:
Truth stands out clear from Error."

MUHAMMAD, SURA 2:256 (ALI)

Fight those who believe not in Allah nor the Last Day,
nor hold that forbidden which hath been forbidden by Allah
and His Messenger, nor acknowledge the religion of Truth,
(even if they are) of the People of the Book, until they pay the Jizya
with willing submission, and feel themselves subdued.

MUHAMMAD, SURA 9:29 (ALI)

When Abu Bakr al-Baghdadi proclaimed his Islamic State in April 2013, he had already been in command of al Qaeda in Iraq (AQI) for three years. Yet despite that fact, his name was not nearly as familiar in the West as that of Osama bin Laden or his own immediate superior, Ayman al-Zawahiri. Since 2013, however, and Baghdadi's subsequent 2014 declaration of an Islamic caliphate, his vastly outnumbered band of fighters has met with stunning success, not only in the war zones of Syria and Iraq, but also in the electronic theater of social media, where thousands of new recruits have been remotely radicalized and mobilized, either to commit lone-wolf attacks in the countries where they live, or to travel to Syria and take up arms with ISIS' savage ranks.

At this writing, estimates of the terror group's numbers vary wildly,[4] from recent U.S. Intelligence figures of about 20,000 fighters, to 200,000, in the opinion of Fuad Hussein, Chief of Staff to Kurdish President Massoud Barzani. A less-disputed estimate by Hussein, in his interview with Britain's The Independent,[5] concerns the territory ISIS controls: "a third of Iraq and a third of Syria with a population of between 10 and 12 million living in an area of 250,000 square kilometres, the same size as Great Britain." Bear in mind that the interview was conducted before ISIS' successful 2015 invasions of Palmyra, in central Syria, and portions of Iraq's Anbar Province, two events which would undoubtedly raise Hussein's estimate.

If you were surprised by ISIS' sudden rise to prominence, you're not alone. Although U.S. Intelligence had listed the pre-ISIS AQI as a threat in early 2007, they were—as their name suggested—still viewed as an al Qaeda subgroup. And even as late as January 2014 the self-proclaimed "state" was dismissed by the White House as relatively insignificant. Moreover, at the time the 2007 threat assessment was issued, ISIS' future "Caliph" was a relative unknown amongst nearly 20,000 prisoners being held at the largest U.S. detention facility in Iraq, Camp Bucca. Described by the news and opinion website *The Daily Beast*[6] as an "unremarkable prisoner [whose] four years at Camp Bucca would have been a perpetual lesson in the importance of avoiding notice," Baghdadi was deemed fit for release and freed in 2009. "I'll see you guys in New York," he said to an American Army colonel as he left the prison, but his words seemed innocuous and no one who heard them recognized the vow he apparently was making.

Still, neither U.S. miscalculations nor the subsequent stunning cowardice of Iraqi troops at Mosul and Ramadi in themselves account for the meteoric rise of ISIS' well-trained, unified army, and their leadership's ability to function politically very much like the "state" they claim to be.

Part of the explanation lies in a label so common that its meaning is often overlooked: ISIS and their ilk are *terrorists.* As much as they claim to "love death more than [we] love life," the truth is their primary goal is to immobilize others through fear. That is why they encourage their fighters to wear action cameras, and have assembled at least one world class media facility. Better than anyone before them, ISIS knows that a television signal blankets more territory than a nuclear bomb ever could. Hence, maintaining their hold on power depends as much on YouTube and "mujatweets" as on swords and mortars.

But much more than a savvy propaganda, political or paramilitary force—the measures used most often inside Washington's Beltway—ISIS must be seen through the paired lenses of history and religious belief by anyone hoping to comprehend, combat and defeat it. It is admittedly difficult to separate the two subjects. Nonetheless, in this chapter we must temporarily set aside the group's religious paradigm and take a look at ISIS' historical family tree. Like most trees, it has roots, a trunk, branches and fruit.

It is deep in the root system that we find our first clues as to ISIS' real goals.

ISLAM'S FAMILY TREE

Muslims, Jews and Christians alike agree that the historical roots of all Middle Eastern peoples, including the radicals who make up ISIS, trace back more than 4,000 years to a Chaldean immigrant named Abraham. But that is where the agreement both begins and ends, with Muslims claiming that Abraham's older son, Ishmael, was the heir whose life God spared on the altar of sacrifice, while Jews and Christians believe that the younger son, Isaac, was the "son of promise." Sadly, the enmity that arose so long ago between the Patriarch's two sons has not only continued for four millennia but— with the advent of Islam in the 7th Century—has intensified, slowly metastasizing like a cancer that drains a body so thoroughly of life that death becomes the goal.

It was in the year 612 A.D. that 42 year-old Muhammad ibn Abdallah abd al-Muttalib, a member of Mecca's dominant Quraysh tribe, proclaimed that he had—by divine revelation—corrected the sectarian split between Judaism and Christianity and had been called to restore the true, unified faith of Abraham, which he called *Islam*, an Arabic term meaning submission.

As in both Judaism and Christianity—if not borrowing from them—Muhammad recognized one true God, whom he called "Allah," meaning literally "the god." The name itself was not new—various Arabian tribes had used it to mean the chief god who had created all the other gods—but Muhammad, who appreciated the growing influence of Jewish and Christian monotheism across the Arabian Peninsula, insisted that Allah was the only god. Not surprisingly, his call to abandon various regional deities and his strict advocacy of daily prayer and other rituals met with local resistance. For one thing, Mecca was an urbanized desert city of traders and wealthy merchants, without the agrarian roots of most Jews and Christians. Muhammad's insistence that his Quraysh brothers should repeatedly prostrate themselves in the dirt before Allah soiled their pride, and his teaching that the wealthy should show generosity to the poor offended their greed.

Such a philosophy, however, had obvious appeal to Mecca's downtrodden servant class, and within a few years Muhammad's followers numbered about seventy families, a large enough sect that the city's elite deemed them a threat and began a wave of persecution that eventually resulted in the group's flight northward some 275 miles to the city of Yathrib.

After having suffered twelve years of rejection and opposition in Mecca, Muhammad was welcomed in Yathrib, where a collection of local converts heralded him as a leader whose message of unity could bring peace to the constantly warring region. Seizing upon the opportunity to formalize his teachings and increase his influence, Muhammad composed what came to be known as the Constitution of Medina.[7] That seemingly benign treaty established inter-tribal peace amongst Yathrib's Muslims, and for a time, with several Jewish tribes living in the area. The uniting of various tribes under a common ideology rather than blood was an unprecedented achievement in the Arab world, and with peace now a demonstrable possibility, the provisions of the Constitution were adopted all across the Arabian Peninsula. Soon, Muslim converts began referring to Yathrib simply as *al-Madinah*, or "the city."

But as his political power increased, Muhammad became vastly less tolerant of dissent. In 623, he organized several raids against Quraysh caravans traveling to and from Mecca, raids which turned into a six-year war when his former tribe began fighting back. Punishments for resisting Islam's Prophet were swift and violent, with decapitation the preferred form of execution. At one point, in 627, he destroyed an entire tribe of Jews, beheading their 700 men and permanently subjugating their 1,000 women and children as slaves.

Finally, in 630, Muhammad led an army of 10,000 troops against Mecca and so overwhelmed the city that he took it without resistance. After cleansing the *Kaaba*—the black cubical shrine that today still serves as the heart of Islam in the center of Mecca's Great Mosque—of its regional idols of the past, the Prophet spent another year consolidating his rule and quashing small pockets of resistance across the peninsula. Then, in 632, he completed his first official *Hajj*, a Great Pilgrimage to Mecca that he had some years earlier prescribed as the duty, at least once in a lifetime, of every able-bodied Muslim.

A few months later, in June of the same year, he succumbed to a fever and died.[8]

It is significant that Muhammad—after he had moved to Medina and become powerful—declared in Qur'an 2:191 that killing his former persecutors had been a sacred duty, since "persecution is worse than killing." Furthermore, in doing so he saw no conflict with his earlier message of peace, which he taught more as the goal of life rather than a pathway to it. After all, he was correcting the past in order to redeem the future, and doing so necessitated constantly striking back at the Quraysh. But in a middle-eastern milieu where ethnic cleansing already had a history among various religions, the Quraysh in turn were bent not only on killing their prodigal but also on annihilating his followers down to the last newborn.

It is no surprise, then, that the Muhammad of Medina would marshal an army. The world as he knew it had always been ruled by regional warlords, and to the Prophet of Islam, Allah would have been perceived not simply as Lord of all the earth, but also as creation's vengeful, political Warlord.

> A Muslim had to redeem history, and that meant that state affairs were not a distraction from spirituality but the stuff of religion itself. The political well-being of the Muslim community was a matter of supreme importance...If state institutions did not measure up to the Quranic ideal, if their political leaders were cruel or exploitative, or if their community was humiliated by apparently irreligious enemies, a Muslim could feel that his or her faith in life's ultimate purpose and value was in jeopardy. Every effort had to be expended to put Islamic history back on track, or the whole religious enterprise would fail, and life would be drained of

> meaning. Politics was, therefore, what Christians would call a sacrament: it was the arena in which Muslims experienced God and which enabled the divine to function effectively in the world. Consequently, the historical trials and tribulations of the Muslim community—political assassinations, civil wars, invasions, and the rise and fall of the ruling dynasties—were not divorced from the interior religious quest, but were of the essence of the Islamic vision.[9]

While the idea of the deity as both redeemer and avenger was nothing new, Muhammad's presentation of the concept in the Qur'an proved problematic, not only for his critics, but also for his successors. Remember, Islam's holy book was claimed to have come directly and exclusively to the Prophet as a "recitation" from the Angel Gabriel, and subsequently transcribed for him by literate friends. But these revelations did not come all at once. Some were penned while the politically powerless Muhammad formulated peaceful Islamic ideals in Mecca, and others later in Medina, where he commanded an army and grappled with the harsh reality of war. As a result, the Qur'an reflects teaching from two drastically different living environments, and as such contains enough variances—contradictions, say its critics—as to render possible two distinctly different versions of Islam, one a religion of peace, as western leaders and diplomats unflinchingly insist, and the other a religion of *jihad*, (holy war), as embraced by extremist groups like ISIS. It is this violent strain of Islam that may be more accurately termed *Islamism*.

THE DNA OF TERROR

So, which claim is true? Did Muhammad give the world a religion of peace? Or did he prescribe the sexual slavery of women and girls, crucifixion of Christians and bisection of babies that have become the grisly signature of ISIS, a band of killers so vile that even al Qaeda has disavowed them?

While these questions will be addressed more fully in succeeding pages, the path taken by Muhammad's immediate successors vividly portrays the answer. Having accepted their founder as the final prophet from God, they found themselves in an awkward situation when it came to matters of authority and administration. Who would replace the Prophet and how would he rule? Certainly, future rulers could not claim divine revelation nor issue edicts with the persuasive weight of Scripture, as Muhammad had done. Instead, as men bound by human limitations, they needed a different, more earthly form of persuasion.

Their solution to the problem, in short, was to finish what their leader had begun: to uproot Muslim identity from the soft soil of spirituality and establish it hard-set in the concrete of statehood. Rather than let Islamic unity splinter back into the tribalism of the past, Muhammad's closest advisors used their influence to successfully promote the election of a supreme leader who would preside over the *ummah* (community) in a combined religious and political role. Hence, the advent of the caliphate—Islam as a nation state—the only divinely sanctioned "nation" in the world, and one whose manifest destiny was to subsume all others.

Thomas Jefferson warned America about this dangerous concept in a 1786, nearly 230 years before there was an ISIS, when he and fellow future President John Adams met with the Ambassador of Tripoli, to try and resolve the growing problem of the Barbary pirates, who were plundering and pillaging American ships, and enslaving U.S. sailors, literally, by the boatload.

> "We took the liberty to make some enquiries concerning the ground of their pretensions to make war upon nations who had done them no injury, and observed that we considered all mankind as our friends who had done us no wrong, nor had given us any provocation. The Ambassador [of Tripoli] answered us that it was founded on the Laws of their Prophet, that it was written in their Koran, that all nations who should not have acknowledged their authority were sinners, that it was their right and duty to make war upon them wherever they could be found, and to make slaves of all they could take as Prisoners, and that every Musselman who should be slain in battle was sure to go to Paradise."[10]

Jefferson's own past study of the Qur'an told him that the ambassador was simply being true to Islamic scriptures, such as Sura 33:26,27:

> And those of the people of the Scripture [Christians and Jews] who backed them (the disbelievers) Allah brought them down from their forts and cast terror into their hearts, (so that) a group (of them) you killed, and a group (of them) you made captives. And He caused you to inherit their lands, and their houses, and their riches, and a land which you had not trodden (before). And Allah is Able to do all things.

The ambassador's citations of this and other suras convinced Jefferson that negotiating with Tripoli and surrounding nations was an exercise in futility, because in the minds of both the ambassador and the Barbary pirates, they were simply appropriating their rightful inheritance according to their holy book. The fact that the ambassador cited the Qur'an, rather than some separate body of the laws of Tripoli, also convinced Jefferson that Islam was a religion whose core values and only authoritative means of expression lay in politics. This was especially true of jihad, the doctrine of holy war that embodied Islam's one sure path to salvation.

Thus, for the next 120 years after Muhammad's death, his various successors increasingly spread their gospel by the tip of the sword, and by the year 750 the Islamic empire stretched from Spain and North Africa to the west as far as today's Pakistan and the border of the Indian Subcontinent to the east. And although it is fair to say that this growth came both through conversion and conquest, it was the threat of the latter that most often produced the former. For whenever politics lifts the sword to command the heart, anyone standing between them will suffer. Jefferson's awareness of this fusion of church and state lay at the heart of his conviction that the two *must* remain functionally separate jurisdictions.

Islam's violent DNA is nowhere more apparent than in the fates of three of Muhammad's first four successors—known as the *rashidun*, or "rightly guided" caliphs—who were assassinated by rivals. In fact, it was a dispute about the fourth Caliph, Muhammad's cousin and son-in-law, Ali ibn Abi Talib, that gave rise to the schism between two groups of adherents that eventually resulted in the two main streams of modern Islam: Sunni and Shi'a.

Immediately following Muhammad's death in 632, the majority of Muslim leaders had wanted to maintain his *sunnah* ("habit" or "usual practice"). They saw succession as the continuity of tradition, meaning that the term "caliph" referred to an office, like the American word, "President." In this Sunni view, the caliph would be appointed either by his predecessor, or if necessary by Islam's senior leaders as a group. (In practice, filling the office soon became a matter of inheritance, effectively rendering the caliph a king.) Today, Sunni Muslims constitute a 75 to 80 percent majority in the Islamic world.

A protesting minority, however, saw succession as the continuity of Muhammad's bloodline, and insisted that since the Prophet had no surviving sons, his son-in-law and cousin, the aforementioned Ali, was his rightful successor. The members of this minority referred to themselves as Shi'a (*shi'atu 'Ali*, meaning "followers of Ali") and claimed that the first three caliphs who succeeded Muhammad were usurpers. Thus, when Ali was finally recognized by the Sunni majority as Islam's fourth caliph in 656, the now-vindicated Shi'a still considered him the first.

Today, Shi'a Muslims (or Shiites) comprise about 20 percent of the world's Muslims, predominating in Bahrain, Azerbaijan, Iran and the southern half of Iraq.

Ironically, from ancient Medina to modern Mosul, terrorist bloodlust has increasingly infected both sides of the divide. "I against my brother; I and my brother against my cousin; I and my brother and my cousin against the world," was for centuries a reliable proverb describing the volatility of Arab tribalism, as every battle invariably boiled down to Sunni versus Sunni, Sunni versus Shi'a, or Sunni and Shi'a versus someone else.

The arrival of ISIS, however, has destroyed the proverb and simplified the proposition: ISIS against everyone. Whether obliterating historical sites or hacking newborns to pieces in their mothers' arms, Abu Bakr al-Baghdadi's holy warriors really do appear to love death—anyone's death—more than they love life. And that is what makes them so incomprehensible, and so able to paralyze their opponents with fear.

ISIS doesn't want to dominate the world. They want to end it.

2

WARRIORS OF THE END OF DAYS

"Black standards will come from Khurasan, nothing shall turn them back until they are planted in Jerusalem."

VOL. 4, BOOK 7, HADITH 2269

It is all too easy for westerners to view Islam monolithically, whether out of bigotry—"they're all alike"—or diplomatically expedient denial—"it's a religion of peace." But the truth about Islam as it has evolved since Muhammad is not reducible to simple sound bites that resemble foreign phrases in a tourist's guide. Instead, gaining even a cursory understanding of it is much like learning a new language.

Just as Roman Catholicism has its hundreds of orders and sub-orders, Orthodoxy its national churches, and splintered Protestantism its myriad denominations, Islam's family tree has more than one trunk, several lesser branches that are invariably influenced by surrounding culture, and countless rebel offshoots. Moreover, the philosophies embraced by the various groups range from Sufist ideations of peaceful coexistence on the one extreme to violent Salafist *jihadism* (a doctrine of holy war) on the other.

The two main trunks of Islam, Sunni and Shi'a, hold much in common philosophically, but with enough disagreement to keep them perpetually at odds. For example, they share the Qur'an, their inviolate Scriptures, as well as the *Hadith,* a collection of teachings and sayings ascribed to Muhammad and allegedly compiled by his trusted friends and advisors. But the two sects differ as to the composition and authority of the Hadith. In fact, unlike the *Torah* of the Old Testament, whose 613 laws comprised ancient Israel's entire legal code, there are six Sunni versions of the Hadith, and three opposing versions in use by the Shi'a. Furthermore, within each version there are three types of Hadith, measured in levels of reliability that, in simplest terms, would be utterly reliable, generally reliable and unreliable, or "weak."

Additionally, both Sunni and Shi'a believe in the *Mahdi,* a prophesied redeemer who will rule at the end of history before the Day of Judgment. But as to the length of the Mahdi's rule and his methods for ridding the world of evil, the two sects differ dramatically. Sunnis believe that he is yet to come, while Shi'a believe that he was born hundreds of years ago and has been kept alive but hidden since his disappearance in the year 872. Both groups believe the Mahdi's arrival will herald a decisive world war and the End of Days, and in recent years both have spawned militant sects who are convinced that through the waging of jihad they can hasten this event.

A third major difference concerns the office of *Imam.* Sunni Muslims use the term to denote any mosque official who functions as a worship leader, teacher and community leader. Shi'a Muslims, however, believe that there have only been twelve Imams—the twelfth being the soon-returning Mahdi of the 9th Century—and that an Imam is an infallible, perfect representation of every aspect of Islam.

But Sunni and Shi'a, while they constitute Islam's main trunks, stand amid a confounding tangle of offshoots and predatory vines, and in order to make sense of the rise of ISIS, it is again necessary to briefly wade into the religion's muddled history.

Few westerners notice, but the Muslim calendar is measured from the time of Muhammad's *hijra* (migration) to Medina in 624. This is significant because it means that Islam traces its beginnings neither to Muhammad's person nor his revelations, but to his political power. As noted earlier, by the time of the Prophet's death in 632, Muslim identity was already shifting from its spiritual base to a political one, and Muhammad's successors were quick to realize that the preservation and expansion of the ummah would necessarily depend more on invasion than persuasion. For one thing, there was little arable land on the Arabian peninsula, and since the Qur'an forbade Muslims to fight one another, the various tribes—having converted—could no longer follow the age-old custom of raiding their neighbors during times of scarcity. Thus, with peace at home only sustainable by aggression abroad, the breathtaking 29-year expansion of the Muslim Empire following the Prophet's demise had less to do with evangelistic fervor than with economic stimulus.

As to whether the Muslim conquerors were ISIS-like oppressors, opinions vary even amongst the most respected historians. Anti-jihadist scholar Robert Spencer, for example, claims that Muhammad himself set a pattern of violence that his successors were bound by their own scriptures to imitate: "in the Messenger of Allah [Muhammad] you have a good example to follow" says Qur'an 33:21. Not true, counters British religious historian Karen Armstrong, "Muhammad was not a man of violence. We must approach his life in a balanced way, in order to appreciate his considerable achievements."[11] Armstrong also insists that the second caliph, Umar, avoided violence and allowed Islam's new subjects to live in peace, building garrison towns for his soldiers, as much to keep the men from pagan corruption as to maintain a strategic presence.

Whether Armstrong is right or not, the challenge of reconciling military duty with Muslim piety proved to be a growing pain the empire could not endure, and in 656 the third caliph, Uthman, was killed in a mutiny that rapidly deteriorated into a civil war pitting his successor, Ali, against one of Uthman's kinsmen, Muawiyyah, Governor of Damascus. The war ended in 661 after a dissident group who considered both men apostate assassinated Ali, and tried but failed to kill Muawiyyah, enabling the latter to take control of the caliphate unopposed.

Muawiyyah consolidated his power in no small measure by moving the Empire's capital from Medina to the recently conquered Damascus, with the goal of transforming the caliphate into a hereditary dynasty named for the Ummayad family of his relative, the late caliph Uthman.

The move to monarchy was met with little resistance by a populace weary of war, save for a minority of devout Muslims who saw the state as monopolizing violence rather than ending it. As a result, Islam, already experiencing a gradually-deepening Sunni/Shi'a divide, suffered further splits amongst the Sunnis, eventually coalescing into two groups: one a mystical movement called *Sufists*, and another claiming to adhere to the ways of Islam's founders, who called themselves *Salafists* (originalists). Yet, even Salafism disintegrated into three subsets, one of which gave rise to the savagery of modern jihadism.

SUFISM

If there is a version of Islam that might once have been called a religion of peace, it would be the Sunni subset known as Sufism, although as with any observation about Islam, there is always an exception.[12] Nonetheless, in historical terms it is safe to say that, whereas Islam in general has focused on external conformity to *Shari'ah* (Islamic law), Sufism has taught that the purification of the soul and mind alone leads to external purity, and that external Islam is but evidence of true inner

Islam. In effect, Sufism strives for that unreachable perfect state wherein Muhammad was able to receive the direct revelation that became the Qur'an.

QUIETIST SALAFISM

Sometimes confused with the Sufis are the so-called "Quietists" of another Sunni subtype, the Salafis, who claim to follow the ways of the "pious Forefathers," a select group that included Muhammad, his companions and followers, and the two generations that succeeded them. The term *salaf* is not new. Just as Christians have from the beginning referred to their first apostles, so also Muslim teachers for centuries have invoked the ideals of their founders, focusing especially on Islam's first three generations because of a saying of Muhammad that is repeated some 74 times in the Hadith:

"The best of you are my generation, and the second best will be those who will follow them, and then those who will follow the second generation,"[13]

Modern Salafism is variously claimed to have originated in 18th Century Arabia, 19th Century Egypt or 20th Century Egypt, depending upon which of the three Salafist strains—Quietists, Activists, Jihadists—is being described. Naturally, all three claim to be most faithful to the ways of their forefathers.

Quietist Salafis shun political Islam in favor of the purification of Islamic religious beliefs and practices, while focusing outwardly on education and missionary work. Quietists also never oppose religious or political rulers, no matter how unjust they may be, because of qur'anic insistence on unity and submission to authority. Such passivity, neither seeking political power nor condemning its abuse, may be one reason why violent groups like ISIS have been able to commit their outrages with so little intramural resistance.

ACTIVIST SALAFISM

Activist Salafis, who also make up a large percentage of the sect, likewise engage in education and missionary work, and eschew violence. But unlike their Quietist brothers, they embrace political involvement, seeing it as a moral and spiritual duty passed down from the Prophet and his pious fellows.

JIHADIST SALAFISM (ISLAMISM)

Jihadists are the third Salafist group, and as is so often the case when cameras are present, they are the belligerent poster child of an otherwise generally peaceful sect. Although they currently comprise a relatively small percentage of the overall Salafist movement, the Jihadist salafis' ranks are growing quickly, and have included the late Osama bin Laden, his al-Qaeda successor, Ayman Al-Zawahiri, and of course, Abu Bakr al-Baghdadi, the leader of ISIS.

(Is is also worth noting that Salafism is the dominant philosophy in Saudi Arabia, where it is called Wahhabism, due to the House of Saud's loyalty to an 18th Century salafist philosopher named ibn Abd al-Wahhab. Practices such as regular Friday beheadings in Saudi Arabia's town squares are routinely and hypocritically ignored by the U.S. for reasons of both economic and political expediency.)

Although they claim to have revived true Islam, groups like ISIS and al Qaeda are rejected by the majority of Muslims worldwide as "modernist" renegades who have broken with 1,400 years of tradition, wherein Muslim universities, schools and madrasas were accepted by the *ummah* as jurists who interpret all aspects of the religion according to scholarly consensus. Instead, ISIS, al Qaeda, al-Shabaab, Boko Haram, the Muslim Brotherhood and similar groups rely heavily, if not almost exclusively, on the teachings of a controversial scholar and logician named Ahmad Ibn Taymiyyah (1263-1328) who rejected any form of consensus beyond that of Muhammad and his companions as "innovation," one of Islam's most egregious sins. Additionally, Ibn Taymiyyah advocated waging war against infidels, apostates and Muslims resistant to his teachings. He also prescribed dismemberment, beheadings, female genital mutilation, the rape of captive women and other violent forms of punishment favored by jihadists groups like ISIS.

In claiming that his group alone is the true *ummah*, ISIS leader Baghdadi is indeed attempting to hijack the Muslim religion of today, as President Barack Obama and other western leaders insist. Yet, there is also a sense in which Baghdadi is merely returning to its original form a religion that he sees as having sacrificed its mandate to subdue all nations in the name of peaceful coexistence. And therein lies the conundrum that keeps much of the Islamic world from denouncing him outright: for on the one hand he is an upstart whose private interpretation of the Qur'an is illegitimate on its face, yet on the other hand seems more faithful to the ways of the Prophet than the authorized majority. In other words, in Baghdadi's mind he is the only marcher in the parade who is in step, and the others—regardless of their unity—are all out of step.

THE PROBLEM OF SHARI'AH

It is the jihadists' unwavering insistence on the literal application of Shari'ah law and its harsh punishments that is the core characteristic of Islamism. "Those who do not judge by what God has sent down are rebellious," says a modern translation of Sura 5:47,[14] and of course rebels must be punished.

Most Americans assume that Shari'ah is a body of laws contained in the Qur'an, but Islam's holy book is only one of four sources of Muslim law, the others being the *Hadith* (collected sayings Muhammad), *Ijma* (prevailing scholarly consensus) and *Qiyas* ("judgment of an act or belief by application of established principles governing some analogous act or belief").[15]

It is the jihadists' rejection of *Ijma* and the use of *Qiyas*—think of street-corner case law—that essentially turns Shari'ah into whatever the mob or black-robed thug on the sidewalk wants it to be. Sadly, a slew of jihadist videos reveals spontaneous trials from Africa to Saudi Arabia and points between, in which unsuspecting pedestrians are stopped, tried for "offenses" as trivial as an unproven accusation of theft, and then punished with 74 lashes, amputation of a limb or even a bullet to the head. Other punishments include immolation, crucifixion, stoning, drowning, beheading (either by sword or explosive necklace) and whatever innovative method promises to terrify locals and enrage the West.

On a larger scale, punishments for ignoring Shari'ah include large munitions,, bombs and ISIS' newest innovation: chemical weapons. According to a Fox News article published in February 2016, "A doctor who was in northern Iraq last year said he treated Kurdish fighters whom ISIS used as 'lab rats for WMD,' and that the variety of burns and illnesses suggested the use of 'mustard gas, precursors, as well as neurotoxic acids.'"[16]

THE MANY FACES OF TERROR

Perhaps no single image so accurately symbolizes Islamic extremism as that of the Hydra, the multi-headed sea monster that guarded the entrance to the Underworld in Greek mythology. ISIS, Boko Haram, the Taliban, Hamas, Hezbollah, various al Qaeda affiliates: Islamic terror seems to have a thousand faces—or at least 82, according to a November 2014 assessment[17] by America's coalition ally, the United

Arab Emirates. And just as in Hercules' attempts to sever Hydra's heads, for each Mideast terror group taken out, two more seem to grow up in its place, with twice the venom of the last. Still, even the most savage groups of the past pale in comparison to ISIS, who, like Hydra, seems to have been bred to be the very watchdog of hell.

How is it that Abu Bakr al-Baghdadi's army so quickly not only took center-stage in the terror world, but seemed to own it as well? And how did the bookish, no-name, former Camp Bucca prisoner manage to proclaim himself caliph—king of the world—and then live to brag another day?

ISIS has been described as the "third wave" of modern jihadism, the first being the guerrilla groups that arose in resistance to the 1979 Soviet invasion of Afghanistan. These *mujahidin* (those who wage jihad), not only forced Russia to spend her way to defeat during the 1980s, but along the way coalesced into various resistance movements. The most prominent of the lot called itself al Qaeda (the camp), and was led and largely funded by a wealthy young Saudi named Osama bin Laden.

After the war, bin Laden spent some years in Saudi Arabia and Sudan, before returning to Afghanistan and establishing several al Qaeda training camps, expanding and strengthening his group until he was able to generate the so-called second wave of jihad, one that crashed ashore on America's east coast on September 11, 2001, with the deadly attacks in New York, Pennsylvania, and Washington, D.C.

More than giving Islamist terror a face, the horrific spectacle of the World Trade Center's Twin Towers disintegrating into a gray dust cloud gave it a logo, a recruitment commercial for global Salafist jihad. It was an idea that for years had amounted to nothing more than campfire chat, but 9/11 brought it to life. Now, terror could become a franchise, and "little people causing big things to fall" a job—complete with a three-page application form[18]—for which disillusioned young men could apply.

Although al Qaeda managed to establish or adopt several affiliate organizations over the next few years, their hopes to replicate the outsize success of 9/11 were never realized. By the time of bin Laden's assassination by U.S. forces in May 2011, the ranks of their leadership had already been decimated, and the organization's influence was clearly on the wane. Nonetheless, the events of 9/11, with its images of the world's only superpower groveling in the dust, had lit a fire in millions of minds. And despite the U.S claim that with bin Laden's demise the war on terror was drawing to an end, the truth was that the world's main stage had been swept clean just in time for the appearance of an even bigger act, already waiting in the wings.

THE RISE OF ISIS

In August 2005, the German website, *Spiegel Online International*, published an article by journalist Yassin Musharbash that gave the West its first glimpse of what is now known as the "al Qaeda 20-Year Plan," which describes the terror network's strategy to establish a worldwide caliphate by the year 2020. The plan includes seven phases:

- Awaken the Muslim world
- Open western eyes to Islam as one community
- Establish al Qaeda as Islam's overlords
- Overthrow hated Arab governments
- Declare an Islamic caliphate
- Provoke an apocalyptic world war
- Establish a permanent, worldwide caliphate

Phase One of the plan, "The Awakening," was claimed to have commenced with the September 11 attacks on Washington, D.C., New York, and Pennsylvania, and would culminate with the fall of Baghdad in 2003, thereby awakening Muslims to the "western conspiracy" against them.

Phase Two, "Opening Eyes," would take three years, and essentially open the eyes of the "western conspiracy" to the *ummah*, Islam as a worldwide community.

Phase Three, "Arising and Standing Up," would last from 2006 until 2010 and "focus on Syria," with additional aggression against Turkey and escalating attacks on Israel. It was the timing of this phase that in April 2006 convinced Abu Musab al-Zarqawi, leader of al Qaeda in Iraq, that "arising" required the declaration of an Islamic State, in effect a caliphate, that July. After Zarqawi was killed by a U.S. joint strike on June 7, his lieutenants proceeded to fulfill their leader's last wish that October, with a hitherto unknown named Abu Umar al-Baghdadi as Islam's "commander of the faithful," a politically convenient euphemism for caliph.

Phase Four should last from 2010 into 2013 and bring about the collapse of hated Arabic governments. And although there is no direct evidence that during that time period an assigned network of jihadis actually coordinated the overthrow of regimes in Egypt, Yemen, Tunisia, and Libya, the televised spectacle of Cairo's "Arab Spring,"—wherein massive throngs overthrew their heavily-armed oppressors with nothing more than cell phones and Twitter feeds—did convince millions of Muslims worldwide that their idyllic Islamic state, the caliphate, was no longer an impossible dream.

Phase Five—remember that the source article was written in 2005—dictated that at this point a worldwide caliphate would be formally declared. "The plan is that by this time, between 2013 and

2016, Western influence in the Islamic world will be so reduced and Israel weakened so much, that resistance will not be feared. Al-Qaida hopes that by then the Islamic state will be able to bring about a new world order."[19]

Whether a true believer or a wily opportunist, it was obvious after the fact that Abu Bakr al-Baghdadi—successor to Abu Umar, who had died in a 2010 air strike—had grabbed bin Laden's bloodied baton and claimed it as his own, thereafter sprinting largely unimpeded and with a prophet's zeal toward the Plan's next goal.

Flouting the proverb that "pride leads to destruction," Baghdadi apparently saw it as a pathway to power, and announced on April 8, 2013 that the Islamic State of Iraq—an al Qaeda branch—was annexing al-Sham (historic Syria), absorbing Syrian jihadist group Jabhat al Nusra, and would henceforth be known as the Islamic State in Iraq and al Sham (ISIS).

The news surprised everyone, especially Jabhat al Nusra, whose leader, Abu Muhammad al-Jawlani, very quickly said thanks but no thanks, as he had already sworn his *bay'a* (allegiance) to bin Laden's successor at al Qaeda Central, Ayman al-Zawahiri. Then real sparks began to fly, with Zawahiri demanding that his rogue subordinate return to Iraq, and Baghdadi responding via audio text that "I have to choose between the rule of God and the rule of Zawahiri, and I choose the rule of God."

At first, Baghdadi's terse response seemed falsely pious, but within weeks the two men's ideological differences began to surface. ISIS was attacking fellow Muslims, claimed al Qaeda, and using *takfir* (the pronouncement of apostasy), far too liberally. Al Qaeda was too soft on Shi'a, too comfortable with democracy, and avoiding jihad, countered ISIS. By February 2014, with various sheiks and al-Qaeda commanders threatening to align with ISIS, Zawahiri issued a statement officially disowning the wayward group.

Baghdadi was unruffled. The momentum was his. Four months later, ISIS captured the Iraqi cities of Mosul and Tikrit.

Phase Six of al Qaeda's Plan, set to commence in 2016, is a period of "total confrontation" between true Islam and the world's infidels. Here, Baghdadi has invoked a hadith that was viewed as prophecy by his mentor, the late Abu Musab al-Zarqawi. Having finally goaded the Western powers into a world war called the *Malahim* ("the battles"), Islam will win its tipping-point victory at a place called Dabiq, in the countryside just north of Aleppo, Syria, 130 miles west of ISIS' headquarters in the city of Raqqa.

Phase Seven sets the year 2020 as a time of "definitive victory" and full commencement of the caliphate.

It is in the plan's sixth phase where ISIS' eschatology (doctrine of last days) comes fully into play. Although the Qur'an lacks detail on the subject, one verse nonetheless places great importance on it: True piety, says its longest *sura*, consists of believing in "Allah, the Last Day, the Angels, the Book, the Prophets" and various acts of generosity and compassion towards fellow Muslims (Qur'an 2:177). Whether or not Muhammad listed these five tenets of Islamic philosophy by priority, that is the way they are interpreted by Muslim fundamentalists (and presumably ISIS). To them, beliefs about the "Last Day" are second in importance only to actual belief in Allah. But where are these doctrines detailed? Not in the Qur'an but in other narrations from the Hadith, Islam's second most authoritative source of instruction.

According to a hadith that quotes a slave named Thawban, "then the black banners will come from the east, and they will kill you in an unprecedented manner.' Then he mentioned something that I do not remember, then he said: 'When you see them, then pledge your allegiance to them even if you have to crawl over the snow, for that is the caliph of Allah, Mahdi.'"[20]

Although ISIS leader Baghdadi has proclaimed a caliphate and named himself caliph Ibrahim, he has not (yet) declared that he is the Mahdi. But the group's black banners and their 2014 push eastward from Syria into Iraq are revealing of their overall goals. In fact, one rendering of the hadith has him saying that the black banners will come from *Khurasan*, an Arabic word that can refer either to the east in general or more specifically to northeastern Iran, the Shi'a Muslim nation that now controls the southern half of Iraq. Thus, ISIS' plain intent to destroy the Shi'a reveals not only historical Sunni hatred for the sect, but also their plan to fulfill prophecy by conquering Iran. For, after the Mahdi's victory at Dabiq, it is from the east that he will begin his sweep westward all the way to Jerusalem. Iran also knows this hadith, and their own moves to counter ISIS in Iraq are proof that they do not intend to allow such a "prophecy" to be fulfilled by anyone else.

It is important to remember that if ISIS is intentionally following al Qaeda's 20-Year Plan, then at some point in 2016 they likely will attempt to initiate a three-year period of "total confrontation" with the West by provoking an all-out Middle East war. But it is also important to remember that with wise action on the part of the West and willing partners in the East, ISIS' version of the End of Days can be proven as mistaken as those that have gone before.

Still, the setting of prophetic deadlines elicits questions: Who grants Abu Bakr al-Baghdadi the authority to make his claims, and why do so many people believe him? And in this instance, what was it about the 20th Century that saw so much of the Middle East transformed into the anti-West?

In short, why do they hate *us*?

3

WHY DO THEY HATE US

"Inshallah [God willing] we will break the barriers of Iraq, Jordan, Lebanon, all the countries...until we reach Al Quds."

Like an ebony mane, Abu Saffiya's curly hair and bushy beard flow from beneath a black baseball cap to wreathe his shoulders. Although the desert sun shines brightly overhead, there is no sweat on the smiling young warrior's brow, and his gray, knee-length pinstripe *kurta* looks dry and freshly pressed, save for a few wrinkles from the leather strap of the rifle slung across his back.

Standing beneath the flag pole at an abandoned border station that until days ago separated the sands of Syria's Al Hassaka Province from those of Iraq's Nineveh Plain, the Chilean jihadist has just replaced the green stars of the Syrian flag with the black banner of ISIS. "There is no nationality: we are Muslims," he says. "There is only one country."

"As you can see, this is under our feet right now," Safiyya brags after stepping onto a toppled metal border sign. "*Inshallah* [God willing] we will break the barriers of Iraq, Jordan, Lebanon, all the countries... until we reach Al Quds [Jerusalem]," he vows, and later dismisses what he refers to as "the imaginary border of Sykes and Picot."

The video Safiyya stars in is, in fact, called *The End of Sykes Picot,* and is a 15-minute propaganda piece that served as ISIS' feature English-language release in celebration of the first day of Ramadan[21] in 2014. In addition to the scenes described above, it includes a display of confiscated vehicles—all American made—as well as a tour of the border's erstwhile headquarters, now a prison holding about 20 former officers and recently captured Yazidi men. The video climaxes with an on-camera explosion of the building, presumably with the prisoners still in it.

But what is "Sykes and Picot" and why is it important enough to appear in the title of an ISIS propaganda film? The answer lies nearly a century in the past, in 1916, near the midway point of World War I.

Although the "War to End All Wars" eventually involved some 135 nations, the main players in 1916 were Britain, France and Russia, allied against Germany, Austria-Hungary and the Ottoman Empire, which encompassed most of today's Middle East. With so many nations involved, it was a given that numerous borders would be redrawn by the victors, and Britain and France in particular were concerned about preserving their Mediterranean trade routes, which were directly threatened by that region's largest political entity, the Ottoman Empire. Thus, they decided, the empire had to go, and with so many internal fractures and tribal conflicts in her past, engineering collapse from within seemed the best path.

To accomplish their plan, the allies dispatched British Intelligence officer T.E. Lawrence from his post in Cairo, Egypt to the Hejaz, the Ottoman-controlled west coast of the Arabian Peninsula, where the Sharif of Mecca, Hussain bin Ali, was eager to launch a revolt against his Turkish oppressors and proclaim his own caliphate. The 26-year-old "Lawrence of Arabia" did a masterful job of wooing Hussain, promising him that once the empire fell, Britain and France would sponsor him to establish a new Arab super-state across "Greater Syria," an area that encompassed what is today Syria, Lebanon, Israel, parts of Iraq and most of Jordan. (ISIS calls this area "al Sham.") Hussain wholeheartedly bought the plan, and the Arab Revolt was under way.

In reality, Britain and France had no intention of honoring their promise. Their goal was to dissolve the Ottoman Empire and permanently fracture the Muslim world, which they believed was necessary to ensure their continued access both to the trade routes and to the region's oil, which was becoming ever more important to western economic success.

Hussain's "activity seems beneficial to us," Lawrence had earlier written to his superiors, "because it marches with our immediate aims, the break-up of the Islamic 'bloc' and the defeat and disruption of the Ottoman Empire....If we can arrange that this political change shall be a violent one, we will have abolished the threat of Islam, by dividing it against itself, in its very heart. There will then be a Khalifa [caliph] in Turkey and a Khalifa in Arabia, in theological warfare."[22]

Lawrence was confident of the plan's success because he viewed the Arabs as administratively inept and historically given to internecine conflict. "If properly handled they would remain in a state of political mosaic, a tissue of small jealous principalities incapable of cohesion and yet always ready to combine against an outside force."[23]

To formalize their collusion, the war departments of Britain and France appointed two men, 37-year old Member of Parliament Sir Mark Sykes and 46-year old French diplomat François Georges-Picot, to draw up a secret agreement that would give each country a post-war sphere of influence spanning most of the Arab world. The shameful reality—and the burning core of today's cauldron of Arab hatred for the West—was that Sykes and Picot simply redrew the maps, creating new countries out of thin air, not basing them upon natural tribal boundaries but purposely breaching those boundaries. The absurdity of modern Iraq, shouldering Shi'a Muslims in the south against Sunni Muslims to the west, and then carving off part of natural Kurdistan to form a northern province, only punctuates the two men's arrogance and presumption. And in the matter of Kurdistan, when asked by the authors why nearly 40 million Kurds were denied nationhood altogether and instead spread across Iran, Iraq, Syria and Eastern Turkey, one highly placed Kurdish leader echoed T.E. Lawrence: to keep the Arab region perpetually destabilized, he said, so it could not cause trouble for the rest of the world.

Such statecraft by the Allies during World War I was both ill conceived and treacherous, as though ethnic cleansing were somehow acceptable if committed by pen rather than sword. Moreover, the scheme underscored western ignorance of the complexity and depth of Middle-Eastern tribalism, which frames Arab social order in much the same way as law in the West, albeit less reliably and with greater resistance to change. Kurds cannot, with a sweep of the pen, simply become Iraqis or Turks, nor can crooked boundaries be straightened with a ruler. The British and French knew this, of course, but badly miscalculated the long-term effect of their presumption. Rather than keeping the various groups at odds with one another, after the war the agreement served to slowly unite them in hatred for the West. "I and my brother and my cousin against the Allies." The "War to End All Wars" had done nothing of the sort, and in fact would prove to be the opening volley in a much longer geopolitical disaster.

The Sykes-Picot Agreement was ratified as the Asia Minor Agreement in May 1916—with the third ally Russia also signing the document—and did indeed include a promise by Britain and France to recognize and protect some form of indigenous governance—perhaps a Confederation of Arab States, or two suzerain kingdoms, one in the British Zone A and the other in the French Zone B. Additionally, the two diplomats had even gone so far as to travel to Mecca, engaging in feigned consultation with the Sharif himself. But the cold truth was that, for the two Western allies, oil ran much thicker than blood.

Even though it was now official, Sykes-Picot must remain a secret—permanently, its colluders hoped, but at least until two other troubling matters were resolved. First, what would U.S. President Woodrow Wilson—who had just won reelection with a campaign slogan, "He kept us out of war"—think of the agreement? And second, what to do with that troublesome little area abutting the Mediterranean coast just north of Egypt, the one called Palestine? Already home to 700,000 people—three-quarters of whom were Arab Muslims—Palestine, with its holy city of Jerusalem, was sacred to Muslims, Christians and Jews alike. Moreover, even before the war, both Britain and the United States had expressed solidarity with Zionist leaders who wanted to reestablish their ancient Promised Land. But Sykes-Picot had been less than clear on that point, and now, failing to address it could undermine its implementation.

The solution to both problems came in the form of a letter from British Foreign Secretary Arthur James Balfour to Baron Walter Rothschild, a prominent Jewish leader who would quickly disseminate it to the Diaspora from Manhattan to Moscow. "The Balfour Declaration," as it came to be known, was published on November 9, 1916, and consisted of a single sentence formally promising that Great Britain would do its best to facilitate the formation of a Jewish homeland along the coast of Palestine, and encompassing Jerusalem. Such a promise, Britain believed, would not only reassure Jews worldwide, but also mollify President Wilson, whose senior White House leadership included at least two fervent Zionists.

Sykes-Picot remained secret for almost a year, only to be exposed in November 1917, one month after Communist pioneer Vladimir

Lenin and his Bolshevik Party staged a successful Russian Revolution. The Bolsheviks, having wrested power from a provisional government formed only nine months earlier after the overthrow of Czar Nicholas II, were furious that Britain and France were suddenly denying Russia's claims in the Ottoman Empire, and they wanted to embarrass their former allies.

Indeed, the sins of the Allies had found them out, as not only various Arab leaders but also the Jews were furious at having been the pawns of their supposed benefactors. The crisis for Britain and France might have been worse, but for the fact that America had at last joined the war in April 1917. Now, the Allies were well on their way to military victory, with or without Russian help, but their veil of moral authority had been torn away.

Within a year the chastened Allies published The Anglo-French Declaration. Clearly written as if to atone for Sykes-Picot, it promised that the two were "one in encouraging and assisting the establishment of indigenous Governments and administrations in Syria and Mesopotamia, now liberated by the Allies, and in the territories the liberation of which they are engaged in securing and recognising these as soon as they are actually established."[24]

On the surface the two declarations appeared to calm the storm, especially after the war had ended and the Arab world had been left at the West's mercies. But in striving to smooth the surface, Great Britain and France had ignored an angry glow beneath it, where a volcano of boiling inner hatred for western imperialism would eventually grow to include the world's new, reigning superpower, America.

WARNING SIGNS

Minor earthquakes provide both warning and relief to seismologists: warning, in that they show where pressure has been building along fault lines, and relief, because they indicate the easing of such pressure. But in quake-prone regions, long periods between the temblors worry the experts, because they know that prolonged silence means a big jolt will eventually come.

It was in the decades following a second World War that, in the West, an ominously silent build-up began. True, there was constant shaking in the lands around the new Mediterranean state called Israel. But even when the tremors became pronounced in 1967 and 1973 their rumblings were still too far away to feel, especially in America, where human suffering was now regularly followed by the weather and sports. As for the deeds of Sykes and Picot, they were names in a book on a shelf in a library somewhere in Paris or London or Boston that was losing out to television anyway. Save for a few private clubs that reeked of cigar smoke and liniment, they might as well never have existed.

Meanwhile, across an ocean and beyond a sea, the pencil marks of Sir Sykes and Monsieur Picot had over the decades etched their way through paper maps and burned through Arab souls, carving ever-deepening fault lines of resentment in the Muslim spirit.

Thus, the treachery continued after the fighting had ceased. Instead of encouraging the formation of free, self-governing states, the Allies had imposed western political structures onto tribalistic societies, producing a new, poisonous nationalism that little by little grew to find its identity more in what it despised than what it valued. Colonels replaced kings, as militaristic regimes arose in the 1950s and 1960s, and by the 1980s had deteriorated into nothing more than brutal dictatorships. By now, the only glue holding T.E. Lawrence's "political mosaic" together was its common hatred for the West.

Little wonder, then, that after 80 years of mounting heat and pressure, a caldera of Islamic hatred erupted so violently on September 11, 2001, and yet again with the fiery 2013 debut of ISIS.

In itself, the group's rebellion surprised no one. Militant Islam has always been a house divided, and after the success of the well-orchestrated Arab Spring revolution in Egypt, Facebook and Twitter had become sandlots in cyberspace, where aspiring jihadis could choose players and form teams for the next series of deadly war games. But what the world did not expect was a full-fledged, uniformed league with a rapidly growing fan base.

Somehow, ISIS has made mayhem attractive and destruction seem romantic. But how? The answer lies in a siren song that since 2014 has seduced thousands of young, would-be dragon slayers and maidens to answer its call.

For those of us in the tone-deaf West, it is time to look carefully at the words.

4

THE LURE OF THE CALIPHATE

No doubt some will bow to the caliphate. Hot heads from across the world will be drawn to this latest craze in theo-pop boy bands.

AFZAL ASHRAF[25]

As an ideal, the caliphate is a universal Islamic state ruled by a legitimate religious and political successor [*khalifa*] to Muhammad. But ideals are elusive things, and like the carrot forever dangling in front of the mule to keep it pulling the cart, it is the lure of the caliphate that has driven fourteen centuries of Muslim longing, from the men of Medina who in 632 huddled in grief to choose their Prophet's successor to today's "caliphettes," runaway girls from Britain and Europe who have been seduced by online promises that they will soon become the brides of heroic ISIS fighters.

Islam has always been torn about the nature of its own existence, especially with regard to political legitimacy. Should it as a "nation" exist only in religious commonality, like Christianity, or should it also possess land and a state apparatus like modern Israel? Muhammad's political stature had been an outgrowth of his religious leadership, but after divine "revelation" died with him his successors saw no choice but to reverse the switch and rely on political force to grow the faith. Hence, a religion in which spiritual conversion and political coercion have nearly always been companions, and today are one and the same in the eyes of ISIS.

Such a mindset mystifies the West, where secularism has for a century occupied the throne of politics. Thus, Abu Bakr al-Baghdadi's sudden proclamation of the Islamic caliphate on June 29, 2014 came as a baffling surprise. Was this a political or religious declaration? He had already carved off portions of Syria and Iraq and declared a new "Islamic State" roughly the size of Great Britain. So why declare a caliphate? And for that matter, asked the masses, what *is* a caliphate?

Government bureaucrats and news reporters the world over scrambled to brush up on their Mideast history and terminology, wondering aloud if Baghdadi's caliphate was real or a calculated stunt, or perhaps just an overblown personal identity struggle.

Meanwhile, the terror leader knew exactly what he was doing: he was saying the magic word. By invoking a caliphate, he was issuing an almost romantic call to arms that he believed would bring a unifying swell to the chests of the disparate bands of Sunni militants wreaking local havoc from London to Lahore.

"[T]here has always been a longing among militant Sunni Muslims, especially Arabs whose countries were artificially divided and dominated by Western colonialism and later by military dictators, for the revival of the caliphate," says Iranian born University of Oxford Professor Farhang Jahanpour. "Even [the] mere utterance of 'Islamic caliphate' brings a burst of adrenaline to many secular Sunnis."[26]

As a recruitment tool, al-Baghdadi's proclamation succeeded. Within weeks, pledges of allegiance to the new caliph were coming from breakaway al Qaeda factions in Yemen and North Africa, the Jama'ah

Ansharut Tauhid group in Indonesia, and Abu Sayyaf in the Philippines. In November, Egypt's powerful Ansar Beit al-Maqdis announced their support in a Twitter audio feed calling on "Muslims everywhere to do the same," and after the new year the vicious Nigerian Boko Haram and Somalian al-Shabaab groups joined the cause.

"I was in a hotel [in the Philippines], and I saw the declaration on television," said Islamic law expert Musa Cerantonio, an influential Catholic-born convert from Melbourne, Australia, in an interview with journalist Graeme Wood for The Atlantic magazine. "And I was just amazed, and I'm like, *Why am I stuck here in this bloody room?*"[27]

Why did invoking the caliphate so intoxicate Cerantonio and his fellow Muslims across such a wide swath of the Arab world?

In a word: territory. A *place* in the world. Rather than calling jihadis to *go* and destroy cities in nations that were not their own, Baghdadi was calling them to *come* and help construct a kingdom of their own.

"The caliphate, Cerantonio told me, is not just a political entity but also a vehicle for salvation," wrote Wood. "[He] quoted a Prophetic saying, that to die without pledging allegiance is to die *jahil* (ignorant) and therefore die a 'death of disbelief.'...The Muslim who acknowledges one omnipotent god and prays, but who dies without pledging himself to a valid caliph and incurring the obligations of that oath, has failed to live a fully Islamic life." Wood responded by saying that such a claim "means the vast majority of Muslims in history, and all who passed away between [the end of the Ottoman caliphate in] 1924 and [the proclamation of Baghdadi's new one in] 2014, died a death of disbelief. Cerantonio nodded gravely. 'I would go so far as to say that Islam has been reestablished' by the caliphate."[28]

Wood's article shook the world of western punditry: Cerantonio, a spokesman for ISIS, was going so far as to say that without physical territory, without a caliphate, Islam itself had been nonexistent for the past 90 years, and Baghdadi's 2014 declaration had resurrected it, but only within the new caliphate's borders. This changed the equation not only for extremists, but constituted a summons to Muslims everywhere: Don't just destroy the unbelievers, he was saying. You are commanded to join us and build Allah's kingdom on earth.

The new caliph had made his announcement in triumphal tones, boasting of fallen flags, demolished crosses, destroyed borders and disgraced *kuffār* (infidels), and rejoiced that "courts have been established... evil has been removed...[and] the religion has become completely for Allah."[29]

But, a singlular collective obligation remained, he added, one that "the *ummah* sins by abandoning."

"It is a forgotten obligation. The *ummah* has not tasted honor since they lost it. It is a dream that lives in the depths of every Muslim believer. It is a hope that flutters in the heart of every *mujāhid muwahhid* (monotheist). It is the *khilāfah* (caliphate)."[30]

For even the most disenfranchised Muslim, such a statement has the ring of truth, which is why Baghdadi said it. Of course he did not expect all Muslims to uproot their families and immigrate to his sand-strewn state—"We will not replace one tyrant by another," the Syrian Muslim Brotherhood growled in response—but that was not his immediate goal in any case. Instead, like a man testing his echo in a cavern, the terror leader was whistling into a particularly large void, one that had cast its hollow gloom across the Middle East for nearly 90 years.

CENTURY OF BETRAYAL

After the end of World War I in 1918 and the implementation of the Sykes-Picot Agreement in 1920, the Middle East awakened, like some hung over sailor, to find itself covered in strange political tattoos. Tribal boundaries had been erased and the Ottoman Empire disintegrated—replaced by a series of odd, straight lines that had nothing to do with the peoples who lived between them. Welcome to the new Middle East.

Two years after Sykes-Picot, the Grand National Assembly of the newly constituted Republic of Turkey abolished the Sultanate and expelled former ruler Mehmed VI, leaving his cousin, Abdülmecid II, to occupy the office of caliph, a position replete with its own treasury and contingent of troops.

New Turkish President Kemal Atatürk, who knew that in Sunni philosophy caliphs embodied the whole concept of political power, rightly saw the threat of a house divided. And as an avowed secularist who considered Islam inherently oppressive, backward and a block to national progress, he took action. In March 1924, the caliphate was abolished and its powers reassigned.

For the first time in centuries, like Rome without its Vatican, the Middle East was without a caliphate. And though it may long have been more myth than reality, its abolition amounted to the toppling of a psychological domino. It should be no surprise, therefore, that during the century since, the rest of the pencil-drawn fictions of Misters Sykes and Picot have gradually dissolved into disarray. Western colonialism, for all its promises of military stability and economic help, has only roiled resentment, and the ensuing decades have seen one pretender after another rise and fall in the name of reviving past glory.

Among the first to collapse after Turkey's restructuring was neighboring Iran (then called Persia), a Shi'a monarchy whose own stability was already being shaken by Russian forces endeavoring to expand their new Soviet Union, and by Britain's efforts to stop them. In 1925, Reza Shah Pahlavi overthrew the Qajar Dynasty that had ruled Iran for 140 years.[31]

Then came a succession of brief kingdoms and military coups, many of them overshadowed by the tornadic cloud of World War II. Yet, even after both Germany and Japan had been defeated and peace had returned to most of the world, the sons of Islam kept swinging their fists, boxing at the shadows of the first great war, raging at a void made all the more insulting by a tiny new presence called Israel on the region's western edge.

"From the campaigns of Kemal Atatürk in Turkey, to the rise of Reza [Pahlavi] in Iran, Gamal Abdel Nasser in Egypt, Muammar Gaddafi in Libya, the military coups in Iraq and Syria that later led to the establishment of the Baathist governments of Hafiz al-Assad in Syria and Abd al-Karim Qasim, Abdul Salam Arif and Saddam Hussein in Iraq, and so on, practically all Middle Eastern countries achieved their independence as the result of military coups," says Jahanpour.[32]

Gaddafi, Assad, Hussein: Independence ideally means the freedom to govern oneself. But in ancient lands that have been ruled from time immemorial by either foreign empires or regional warlords, modern independence has brought one exploitative, cruel dictatorship after another. And the savagery of Baghdadi's Islamic State caliphate already appears to have eclipsed them all, for "freedom" in the caliphate means only the freedom to live in mortal fear under Shari'ah law.

As a matter of Islamic history, there had almost always been some sort of caliphate—if not rival ones—somewhere. And just as Christendom split first into East and West, and subsequently splintered into national churches and myriad denominations, so Islam began as one and then progressively fractured—nearly always violently—along the way.

The predominantly Christian West has known its episodes of violence, of course, but thanks to a concept of law generally grounded in covenants and treaties, such conflict has sporadically marked the trail of history more than it has lined it. Likewise, a religious heritage that emphasized looking to the future for the appearance of a divine kingdom contributed in no small measure to the West's philosophy of historical progress, industry and innovation.

In stark contrast, ever since Mongol invaders laid siege to Baghdad in 1258 and put an end to 500 years of the Muslim Empire's growth and prosperity, Islam's ummah has looked to the *past* for its model of perfection. Indeed, ISIS' modernist adaptation of what it calls the "Prophetic Methodology" is an appeal to the perceived superiority of 7th-Century life under the rule of Muhammad. Far from a nostalgic longing for the simplicity of bygone days or even pride in their heritage, Muslims in general and the leaders of ISIS in particular view their religion's beginnings as a struggle every bit as heroic and divinely blessed as David's victory over Goliath or Israel's miraculous crossing of the Red Sea. The future, however, has remained an elusive, shrouded ideal.

More than a matter of new borders, the implementation of Sykes-Picot at the end of World War I was an attempt to impose upon the Arab world a 300-year old Western concept of nationhood called Westphalianism. A century after German theologian Martin Luther had triggered the Protestant Reformation, Europe was mired in a series of regional religious wars that eventually led to the Thirty Years' War, a Protestant versus Catholic conflict that engulfed nearly all of Central Europe from 1618-1648, killing millions of Europeans in the process.

Finally, over a five-month period from May-October 1648, representatives of the Holy Roman Empire and various Protestant nations signed a series of peace treaties that collectively came to be known as the Peace of Westphalia, the region of Germany where the signings took place. Although the treaties did not bring immediate peace to all of Europe, they did establish principles of national sovereignty, non-interference and religious self-determination that eventually became—and remain—foundational to international relations amongst the world's major powers.

The brutal hypocrisy of the Sykes-Picot Agreement was that it violated the Westphalian principles it sought to impose, and as a consequence awakened not only a thirst for revenge amongst the Muslim warrior class, but also the deeper, nearly universal Muslim dream of the caliphate, with its promise of national identity, personal self-respect, material blessing, and economic and political might.

"Even if the divisions within the Arab world make a caliphate seem impossible to achieve," says Cambridge University's John Casey, "very many Muslims—perhaps the majority throughout the world—respond to it instinctively as an ideal. A leader who with God's blessing dispenses law and justice throughout the countries of Islam appeals as profoundly to the Muslim imagination as the kingdom of Christ upon earth or St Augustine's City of God did to Christians in Europe for at least 1,500 years...So you can understand why young men can be dazzled by the idea of a caliphate—by something that claims to embody ancient ideals and to avenge recent humiliations."[33]

Adding to ISIS' promise to exact revenge and establish Allah's kingdom on earth is a third factor that has contributed greatly to the group's growth and quickly maturing state apparatus: pragmatism.

ISIS, for all its ferocity, is Sunni, while Iraq's ruling National Alliance party members are Shi'a. And in a country where Shi'a outnumber them nearly two to one, many Iraqi Sunnis prefer Baghdadi, the devil they only recently met, to the Shi'a one they know all too well.

Before ISIS crashed her western border and grabbed a sizable chunk of northern and western Iraq, then-Prime Minister Nouri al-Maliki, with Iran's help, had for eight years attempted to consolidate Shi'a power in Baghdad by disenfranchising Iraq's Sunni and Kurdish minorities at every turn.

"The principal error made in the postwar years was the immediate banning of all members of Saddam's Ba'athist party," writes journalist Benjamin Hall. "No former Ba'athists were allowed to join the newly established Iraqi army...and as a result the country was left in the hands of people with little experience, while many disgruntled Ba'athists lost everything. Thousands were left jobless: teachers, doctors, professors, and soldiers were all banned from holding public sector positions because they had joined Saddam's party— which had been practically imperative under his regime. They found themselves unable to support and feed their families, and their anger grew to the point that joining Sunni terrorist movements in the west of the country seemed to be the only alternative—the only way to change their downfall."[34]

One such movement was al Qaeda in Iraq, from whose ranks the renegade Baghdadi formed ISIS, then the Islamic State and eventually his caliphate. Yet even while ISIS was still AQI, many of Saddam's old Ba'athist cronies had quietly pledged their personal loyalty and governmental expertise to Baghdadi. Two of them, Abu Ali al-Ansari and Abu Muslim al-Turkmani, served as Baghdadi's top advisors, with Ansari overseeing Syria until his death in November 2014 at the hands of Kurdish forces, and Turkmani in charge of Iraq until his death by an American drone strike in August 2015.

A third formerly high-ranking Ba'athist—he was the King of Clubs on the U.S. military's most-wanted Iraqi playing cards—is Izzat Ibrahim al-Douri, who once acted as Army vice-chairman on Saddam Hussein's Iraqi Revolutionary Command Council. Douri managed to evade capture by American forces after the overthrow of Saddam in 2003, and went on to lead the now-banned Baath Party, while also forming his own army, The Army of the Men of the Naqshbandi Order. Douri[35] and his troops are thought to have been the key to ISIS' successful takeovers of the Iraqi cities of Tikrit and Mosul in 2014.

Thus, while ISIS' spectacular invasion of Iraq in June 2014 was a shock to much of the world, in reality the terror group had already established enough organizational momentum not only to take territory but to keep it. And it is the group's apparent staying power that has caused many Iraqi Sunnis to seek safety in the caliphate.

Even Raghad Hussein, daughter of the late Saddam Hussein, now living in Jordan, is an ISIS supporter, one who is suspected of using her considerable fortune to finance at least some of their ventures. "I am happy to see all these victories," Hall reports her as saying shortly after ISIS' successful invasion of Mosul. "Someday, I will return to Iraq and visit my father's grave. Maybe it won't happen very soon, but it will certainly happen."[36]

Such is the lure of ISIS' caliphate, holding out not only a guarantee of retribution and reparations for past injustice, but beyond that the restoration of an empire that promises to become more glorious than any Promised Land or Shining City on a Hill. Abu Bakr al-Baghdadi knows this, and whether or not he truly believes it, he knows the appeal it holds for an Arab world long shamed, one that hungers for revenge and craves respect. Even more dangerous, he knows that his caliphate ideal is infused with what young people the world over find themselves lacking: *purpose*. Whether to Arab youth, alienated by the hypocrisy of obscenely wealthy sheiks who give lip service to Islam while bathing in the Great Satan's oil money, or to young westerners whose only heroes live in movies and whose kingdoms are Disney-branded and paved with plastic trees, purpose is a fantastic lure.

Literally fantastic.

For while Saddam's daughter may or may not ever achieve her wish of returning to Iraq, there are other men's sons and daughters, from all over Europe, England, and as far away as the USA, who are making the fateful journey to join the ISIS caliphate. Most are much younger than Raghad Hussein. In fact, not too long ago many of them were still watching fanciful cartoon depictions of Arabian princes like Aladdin, and dreaming of magic carpet rides. Now, they are boarding jets that will take them first to Istanbul and then on to Syria, to fulfill a grander fantasy of becoming the valiant young warriors and brides of the caliphate. Tragically, whether they know it or not, for nearly all of them it will be a one-way trip.

5

SEDUCING CALIPHETTES

Mélodie stares into her computer screen,
admiring the strong man eighteen years her senior.
She loves him, even if she's only ever seen him on Skype.

"Do you really love me?" Mélodie murmurs,
her voice childish and frail.

"I love you for the sake of Allah. You are my treasure,
and the Islamic State is your home. Brick by brick,
we'll build a better world...."[37]

The words of ISIS fighter Abu Bilel are as sweet as honey, and 20-year old Mélodie of Toulouse, France feasts on them. For the first time in her life she feels loved. Not that her mother and sister don't love her—of course they do, but this is different. This is a man's love, infused with a vision and purpose the fatherless young woman has never known. Bilel is strong, desirable, passionate and brave. He is her knight, her Arabian knight, and already Mélodie feels her soul soaring towards Syria, as if borne on Aladdin's carpet, to join him in the caliphate.

Bilel is lying, of course, as he has been for the past ten days and will for the next twenty, when he will discover that his sweet Mélodie is no more real than the ludicrous fantasy his lust has compelled him to spin.

Mélodie, in fact, is the Facebook avatar of Anna Erelle,[38] a 30-year old French journalist investigating what she calls "Jihad 2.0", the social media channels through which ISIS so successfully seduces and mobilizes surprisingly large numbers of European teens to join their deadly cause. But Erelle has caught a bigger fish than she intended when, only a few days ago as Mélodie, she "shared" one of Bilel's boastful videos on Facebook. None other than the right hand man of ISIS' self-anointed caliph, Abu Bakr al-Baghdadi, Bilel saw the girl's post and his ego has gotten the better of him. And for the next three weeks, in an effort to woo the sweet, gullible Mélodie, whose beautiful eyes sparkle between the slits of a black veil that guards her identity during their Skype calls, he will betray ISIS' wickedly effective recruiting secrets in real time.

Unlike Erelle's fictional Mélodie, whose flirtation with a terrorist ended with a cancelled Skype account, Canadian Damian Clairmont's exposure to militant Islam was more direct. A purportedly happy child until his father left the family when he was 10 years old, Damian wrestled with depression thereafter, retreated to his computer, and even attempted suicide not long before converting to Islam at age 17.[39]

"And I was completely open to that because I told him when he was young, [faith is] going to be a matter of personal choice, it has to be something that's right for you," his mother, Christianne Boudreau said, adding that at first she liked the changes she saw in him.[40] But after her son began attending prayer services at a Calgary mosque, he grew distant, not only observing Muslim customs but openly rejecting his family's Western ways.

Not long after turning 21, Damian told his mother he was going to Egypt to study linguistics, but three months later she learned that he had gone to Syria to join the jihadi group, Jabat al-Nusra. A short time later, the young man switched his allegiance to ISIS leader Baghdadi.

In January 2014, Christianne Boudreau received a text from Syria, informing her that her son had been killed in a battle near Aleppo, Syria.

NOT INSANE: DEVOTED TO A "HIGHER" CAUSE

If Baghdadi and company were simply some 21st-Century version of a Bedouin gang, car-bombing and plundering their way across the desert from one mortar-pocked town to the next, they would at least be somewhat comprehensible to average European and American news watchers. Over the past few decades before ISIS, the West had grown uneasily accustomed to modern Mideast terrorism, and to the condescending punditry that ascribed it to economic frustration, educational deprivation and a general lack of cultural sophistication. Such flawed analysis provided false comfort in the years immediately following 9/11, since figuring the terrorists out *felt* like a logical first step to stopping them.

But the arrival of ISIS, with its slick, sickening videos of prisoners in orange jumpsuits exploding into clouds of pink mist, complete with slow-motion replay, stopped the West's spin game like a jarred pinball machine. Pundits tilted. Diplomats lied. Leaders failed to lead. And news networks added priests and psychologists to their rosters.

Individuals who commit atrocities are quickly labeled mentally ill. "No sane person is capable of this," say the TV analysts, and millions of sane persons vigorously nod in agreement, assuring themselves that neither they nor their children have the capacity for such degeneracy. But ISIS is *thousands* of men and women, some still in their mid-teens, who seem determined that each atrocity will be more perverse than the last, with better special effects. And while psychologists try day after day to explain this evil in five-minute television segments designed for adults, ISIS churns out an average of 90,000 posts per day on social media sites like Twitter and YouTube, where they continue to grow an alarmingly young following on smartphones, tablets, and bedroom laptops around the world.

What kind of young person is drawn into this macabre web? Is it only the lonely Mélodies and disaffected Damians, or could your normal, well-adjusted child be a target? The answers are yes and yes. As in any successful advertising campaign, ISIS first qualifies its customers and then carefully tailors its approach. And the Internet makes the process easier than ever.

"A decade ago al Qaeda would meet potential recruits face to face; now ISIS engages in one-to-one dialogue while [sitting] 2,000 miles away," says Scottish attorney and antiwar activist, Aamer Anwar.[41] who represents the family of infamous ISIS poster girl, Aqsa Mahmood, who in November 2013 ran away from her Glasgow home and went to Syria, where three months later she was wed to a jihadi fighter.

Citing the way many young British Muslims are able to hide vices like underage drinking and illicit sex from their parents, Anwar says that recruits like Aqsa are just as easily able to hide their digital footprint and budding interest in jihad. Further, when they do announce an interest in the Muslim religion, their parents are happy, and often given to a false sense of security.

"The failure to deal with the grooming of underage girls by ISIS is a child protection issue," he says. "When a paedophile makes contact with a child, he builds up trust over several months, convincing the child not [to] discuss anything with her parents. When the time is right he convinces the child to leave her family and join him. The process is identical in radicalization by ISIS."[42]

Anwar's observation is confirmed in cases like that of 23-year old Alex, a lonely and emotionally immature young woman who lived with her grandparents in rural Washington state. The subject of a 2015 New York *Times* interview,[43] Alex earned spending money working two days a week as a babysitter and teaching Sunday school. Isolated in her grandparents' country home for the rest of the week, she spent hours watching Netflix movies and interacting with the outside world via social media and smartphone alerts, which was how she learned of the beheading of American journalist James Foley in August 2014.

"Riveted by the killing, and struck by a horrified curiosity," according to the *Times*, Alex logged onto Twitter and soon found herself in communication with users claiming to be members of ISIS, who politely answered her questions and then, in suitably chatty tones, began asking about her life. Within a short time she was befriended by a man named Monzer Hamad, who said he was an ISIS fighter stationed near Damascus, Syria.

At first, Monzer engaged in small-talk with Alex, taking an interest in her and sprinkling his replies with plenty of youthful LOLs and emoticons. Then, after two months, he began encouraging her to reread her Bible and to read the Qur'an, pointing out similarities between the two, while also showing how Islam had corrected Christianity's mistakes. After Monzer's texts suddenly ceased in October, a British man named Faisal took his place as her tutor in Islamic teachings.

Alex converted on December 28, 2014, posting her declaration of faith to her Muslim following on Twitter. Within minutes, congratulations began pouring in from "brothers" and "sisters," terms that brought Alex, an only child, to tears. A few days later in January, packages of gifts began arriving from England: a green prayer rug, pastel-colored hijabs, books, and in every box some bars of Lindt™ chocolate, in honor of a brother—Faisal explained—who had killed two infidels in a Lindt™ Chocolate Cafe in Australia.

Now, Alex was living a double life, keeping her hijab hidden in her truck for trips away from home, while still teaching Sunday school and babysitting. Not having met any fellow Muslims in real life, she started to attend a nearby mosque, but Faisal warned her that its leaders were against jihad. Her inner turmoil and sense of isolation were growing worse now, and it showed in her posts. A few Twitter followers, recognizing the signs of radicalization, began warning her of the trap into which she was being drawn, while at the same time her jihadi suitors started demanding that she break ties with her Christian friends and all online *kuffar* (infidels).

In March, Faisal told Alex she needed to find peace in a Muslim land and that he had found her a husband. He offered to buy her airplane tickets to Austria, where she could meet the man and enjoy a holiday before continuing on to her unspecified new homeland. She might have made the fateful journey, but for the fact that her now-wary grandparents confiscated her computer and discovered the truth.

After learning that Faisal was a 50-something married man and father, who had served time in a Bangladesh prison for running a bomb-making factory, Alex agreed to break ties with him. Her grandparents then closed all her social media accounts, except for Skype, which they forgot. Soon afterward, she resumed contact with Faisal, and as of June 2015, was still exchanging messages with him.

Alex's openness with the *Times* reporters was unusual, as was that of the Scottish teen, Aqsa Mahmood, who kept a public blog and wrote very transparently about her conversion from "normal" western teenager to militant ISIS bride. In a September 11, 2014 blog entitled *Diary of a Mujahirah*, she wrote:

"The media at first used to claim that the ones running away to join the Jihad as being unsuccessful, didn't have a future and from broke down families etc. [sic] But that is far from the truth.

"Most sisters I have come across have been in university studying courses with promising paths, with big, happy families and friends and everything...If we had stayed behind, we could have been blessed with it all from a relaxing and comfortable life and lots of money."[44]

Other than being willing to talk freely about their conversions, Alex and Aqsa are in every way opposites: one a Scottish teen from an urban, middle-class, moderate Muslim family, happy and outwardly well-adjusted; the other a lonely American country girl, raised by Christian grandparents and teaching Sunday school. But ISIS recruiters knew how to reach both young ladies with promises of romance, domestic bliss, a life full of meaning, membership in a just cause, and for especially naïve prospects like Alex, even chocolate.

LIFE IN "PARADISE"

"When you come to live with me, you'll see what a paradise me and my men are building. You'll be amazed. Here, people care about each other. They respect each other. We're one big family, and we've already made a place for you— everyone is waiting for you!"[45]

Abu Bilel's promises to the fictional Mélodie are standard fare for ISIS recruiters who prey on women and girls in the West, and hundreds have taken the bait, making the fateful journey to the jihadists' "paradise" in Raqqa, Syria. What they encounter after arriving, however, is a city turned virtual prison, where executions take place in the city square every Friday, and where the slightest female "sin"—such as wearing perfume or even raising one's voice—can provoke a lashing or worse. From day one they are covered head-to-toe in black, and can never leave home without permission. As for marriage, most European girls are vetted, trained and assigned spouses within a few weeks, but many find themselves "married" to one fighter for a week, then divorced and married to another the next week, and so on. Kurds, Iraqi Christians and especially Yazidis are treated even worse, with girls as young as six years old raped and beaten, often several times a day,[46] while others are sold at market in order to help finance the caliphate.

SEX, LIES AND ALTRUISM

The terror group's approach with young male recruits is equally calculated but more daring, with appeals to the adolescent thirst for adventure, sexual lust and, as in Damian Clairmont's case, an assurance that they can join a heroic fight to restore justice to an unjust world. The predators are also patient and willing to work slowly, rewiring their candidates' psyches and values remotely, like a surgeon performing arthroscopy with a fiber-optic camera.

"Bit by bit, it wasn't anything drastic that would stand out, but slowly over a period of time starting in 2011, he grew his beard and cut his hair really short," said Damian's mother.

"He started talking about how the media was portraying the lies about what was really happening around the world. He said we didn't know the truth here and that the Western world was selfish....Then he became more rigid over wine at the table—whereas before he would respect that, even if he didn't drink. Then, all of a sudden, he wouldn't even come to the table."[47]

Julia Joffe, the reporter who interviewed Damian's mother, also spoke with German deradicalization expert, Daniel Koehler, who said Damian's case had followed a "classic radicalization process."

"First, the recruit is euphoric because he has finally found a way to make sense of the world. He tries to convert those around him—and, in the case of radicalized Muslims in recent years, to make them care about the suffering of Syrians. The second, more frustrating stage comes when the convert realizes that his loved ones aren't receptive to his message. This is when the family conflicts begin: arguments over clothing, alcohol, music. At this point, the convert begins to consider advice from his cohorts that perhaps the only way to be true to his beliefs is to leave home for a Muslim country. In the final stage, the person sells his possessions and often pursues physical fitness or some kind of martial training. As his frustration mounts, his desire to act becomes overwhelming, until he starts to see violence as the only solution."[48]

In addition to appealing to the male sense of adventure and altruism, there is carnal pleasure, a secondary but nonetheless important factor in ISIS' recruitment of idealistic western males—including the so-called "lone wolves"—and one that has long been used to motivate Islamic terrorists in the Arab world, as the New York *Times* reported in August 2015.

"In the moments before he raped the 12-year-old girl, the Islamic State fighter took the time to explain that what he was about to do was not a sin. Because the preteen girl practiced a religion other than Islam, the Qur'an not only gave him the right to rape her—it condoned and encouraged it, he insisted.

"He bound her hands and gagged her. Then he knelt beside the bed and prostrated himself in prayer before getting on top of her.

"When it was over, he knelt to pray again, bookending the rape with acts of religious devotion."[49]

From whence does ISIS derive what the article terms a "theology of rape"?

"Also (forbidden are) women already married, except those (captives and slaves) whom your right hands possess," begins Qur'an 4:24,[50] a sentence which ISIS and other terror groups interpret as legitimizing rape during wartime, while more moderate Islamic spokesmen insist that it references consensual sex only. But the idea of having consensual relations with a recently-captured woman is ludicrous on its face, and indeed an explanation of the verse, directly from the Hadith, lends itself easily to the wartime theory.

> "Abu Sa'id Al Khudri said 'The Apostle of Allah sent a military expedition to Awtas on the occasion of the battle of Hunain. They met their enemy and fought with them. They defeated them and took them captives. Some of the Companions of Apostle of Allah were reluctant to have relations with the female captives because of their pagan husbands. So, Allah the exalted sent down the Qur'anic verse, "And all married women (are forbidden) unto you save those (captives) whom your right hand posses [SIC]." This is to say that they are lawful for them when they complete their waiting period'" (Abi Dawud, English Book 11, Hadith 2150).[51]

Rape during wartime is much more than a sexual outlet, of course. It is also a weapon of fear, submission, revenge and humiliation, and the command structure of ISIS knows this all too well. Yet, the sexual aspect of rape also infuses the extremist mentality in a way unknown in the west, because in jihadist belief non-consensual sex (i.e., relations with *houri*, heavenly servants who possess no will at all), is a precursor to Paradise (*Jennah*) itself.

WHERE VICE IS VIRTUE

The idea of an orgiastic heavenly abode as a feature of Islamic belief is rarely mentioned in western media, where it is a politically incorrect subject referenced only by the more irreverent pundits, usually in the form of a dismissive one-liner about suicide bombers seeking their "72 virgins." But the Qur'an devotes much attention to eternity, with "a reference, direct or indirect, to one aspect or another of the afterlife on almost every single page," according to the Muslim website *islamicity.org*, and often uses phrases such as "if you believe in Allah and in the afterlife," as though the two are a single belief. It should be no surprise, therefore, that the Qur'an also addresses the subjects of marriage and sexuality in the hereafter.

It is a hadith considered "weak" by Islamic scholars, not the Qur'an, which references 80,000 servants and 72 wives in Paradise, but since the Hadith claim to be sayings of the Prophet as told to or overheard by his associates, this reference is still enthusiastically received amongst the deviants who comprise ISIS' army.

As for the Qur'an's infallible depiction of Paradise, it is a place—for men at least—of unimaginable rewards, with endless feasting, inexhaustible wealth and unlimited wishes come true. In short, sins of the flesh such as gluttony, greed and promiscuity are virtues in heaven. In Jennah, believers will be young and beautiful, served by "immortal youths (*houris*) with jeweled and crystal cups filled with the purest wine which will neither give them headache nor hangover, with fruits and meats of their desire. They will be fair ones with lovely intense eyes like guarded pearls; A reward for the good deeds of their past life" (Qur'an 56:17-24). Moreover, Allah has created these servants as "mates for them and made them virgins, matched in age, for the companions of the right hand" (vv. 35-38), who will be forever "chaste, restraining their eyes in modesty, never touched by man or Jinn [English *genie*, i.e., a spirit of lower rank than an angel]" (v. 56).

Muslims receive these promises as divine revelation, while secular scholars hypothesize that Muhammad's concept of Jennah was largely borrowed from the religion of Zoroastrianism—the pre-Islamic religion of Iran—especially with regard to the Qur'an's *houri* and a spirit being in Zoroastrianism called the *Daena*, a beautiful female being said to accompany the soul of the departed to Paradise. Whether or not Islam's critics are correct in this assessment, the Qur'an nevertheless presents Jennah as a place where every believer, with every conceivable human appetite sated beyond imagination, is surrounded by eternally-virginal, amorous companions. Likewise, the Hadith, taken as a whole, quotes Muhammad as expounding on these companions in quite lurid terms. ISIS and other jihadi Salafists have in turn acted on them in increasingly inhumane, downright beastly ways, some of them unprintable in a book written for the general public.

This explains why sexual torture and rape are not just anomalies or the tragedies of war, but are actually held in high regard by Islamic extremists like the Taliban, al Qaeda and their successor, ISIS.

GUERRILLAS IN THE MIDST

With social media providing a potential doorway into any home via computers and smartphones, ISIS has been able to successfully radicalize a stunningly broad array of recruits, from impressionable country girls and urban idealists to the most vile and maladjusted of the world. Worsening the problem in the West has been the sheer naïveté of an older generation—especially parents of adolescents—who think of handheld electronic devices as nothing more than handy gadgets for calling home, watching movies and playing video games. But in truth, today's smartphone is more powerful than yesterday's supercomputer, and that fact, along with most young people's unfettered access to the same cyberspace routinely prowled by ISIS, makes the device easily as dangerous to their children as whiskey and car keys.

ISIS has also changed the social media rules of engagement. Just as colonial America's Minutemen ignored conventional battle techniques in order to defeat Britain's best in the 18th Century, so ISIS is redefining Western concepts of the human capacity for evil. Especially problematic is the politically-correct but wrongheaded game—being played everywhere from the statehouse to the schoolhouse—of religious moral equivalency. Any public figure, whether in business or politics, who criticizes militant Islam is expected also to acknowledge the skeletons in the closest of Judaism and Christianity.

More specifically, the dictates of political correctness make it a virtue for Judeo-Christian societies to criticize themselves—if not confess to being the very cause of ISIS—and blasphemous to criticize Islam or to claim that the terrorists are in any way authentically Muslim. The result is a diplomatic and strategic paralysis that reduces western governments to gawking from the sidelines of a very deadly game.

6

DID WE CAUSE ISIS?

"When you don't call things by their real name, you always get in trouble."

THOMAS L. FRIEDMAN

"Change is the only constant," Heraclitus of Ephesus is reputed to have said in acknowledging the unpredictability of life some five centuries before the birth of Jesus. But the Greek sage might as well have been describing the western world's frustration in dealing with the post-9/11 Middle East. From al Qaeda's surprise attacks on the American homeland in September 2001 to Russia's sudden power grab in Syria in 2015, time after time the U.S. appears to have been taken off guard, slow to respond and, when finally doing so, as clumsy as a child playing Whack-a-Mole, an arcade game where the object is to hammer moles that randomly pop up and down from holes on a platform.

After a ten-year search, President Barack Obama succeeded in finding and permanently "whacking" al Qaeda leader Osama bin Laden on May 2, 2011.

Pop. Al Qaeda prodigal Abu Bakr al-Baghdadi established ISIS in 2013.

They're just a "jayvee squad," said President Obama in January 2014.

Pop. Five months later, ISIS conquered Mosul, Iraq's second largest city.

Inundated with 600,000 Syrian and Afghan refugees in 2015, Europe's leaders huddled with Canada and the U.S. in trying to cope with the flood.

Pop. Russia's opportunistic President Vladimir Putin sneaked jets into Syria and gave America one hour to clear the skies before his forces began a bombing campaign that would surely worsen the exodus.

Heraclitus probably would have loved Whack-a-Mole.

How did this malignant mess happen? Was it because one President took us into the region, or because his successor pulled us out? Or, did the spark of the 9/11 attacks ignite a Middle East explosion that had been brewing ever since Sykes/Picot?

Regardless of whether someone's bad politics is to blame or not, there is no denying that since al Qaeda's American debut in 2001, the world has gone very wrong, especially with the advent of ISIS, which has destabilized the entire Middle East and succeeded in knocking the West so far off its axis that any attempt at recovery risks making things worse. Adding to the danger, other mischief makers such as Iran's Ayatollah Khamenei and Russia's Vladimir Putin are triangulating like hyenas at a lion kill, hungry to grab a few pieces of nearly-dead nations for themselves.

Reckoning with this awful reality after expending so much blood, effort and resources demands a search of the national soul. And of all the questions that arise from such introspection, there is one more terrible than all the others:

Did we cause ISIS?

The view in the rearview mirror may not be pleasant, but it is clearer than the road ahead and thus worth a serious look back.

AFGHANISTAN

Before invading Afghanistan, President George W. Bush issued an ultimatum to that country's Taliban government: Hand over the terrorists, or share in their fate. Since the whole world knew well that Afghanistan's leaders were themselves terrorists and would never cooperate, the demand was a formality. On October 7, 2001, the U.S. officially launched Operation Enduring Freedom, a four-phase war plan that, according to Bush's post-presidency memoir, *Decision Points,* would first target al Qaeda and the Taliban, then conduct humanitarian airdrops to the Afghan people, thirdly deploy American and allied ground troops to hunt down remaining Taliban and al Qaeda fighters, and finally stabilize the nation and help the Afghan people build a free society.[52]

Routing the Taliban with air strikes took a mere five days, and seven weeks later, on December 21, Afghanistan named a new interim President, prominent tribal leader Hamid Karzai. Osama bin Laden, however, along with other al Qaeda and Taliban leaders, had escaped across the mountains into Pakistan, where most would take refuge for the next several years. Bin Laden was killed in May 2011, of course, but neither al Qaeda nor the Taliban have met such a fate at this writing. In fact, far from being "decimated" at its core, as President Obama claimed in 2012, al Qaeda was "morphing and franchising itself not only here but other areas of the world," according to subsequent testimony by U.S. Director of National Intelligence James Clapper, before the Senate Armed Services Committee in February 2014.

As for the Taliban, they knew that from Alexander the Great in the 3rd Century BC, to Britain in the 19th Century and the Soviet Union a century later, no occupying power had ever successfully remained in

Afghanistan, the "Graveyard of Empires." In fact, the Soviet effort, which lasted from 1979-89, not only failed miserably but actually galvanized the Afghan rebels and also forced them to organize, directly contributing to the formation of al Qaeda.

Thus, the Taliban waited, quietly rebuilding their ranks and beginning a new insurgency while the rest of the world focused first on al Qaeda and then ISIS. By the fall of 2015, the Taliban's numbers had grown larger than they were before the 2001 U.S. invasion, and they were causing such widespread turmoil that President Obama, in a complete turnabout from previous policy, announced that some 5,500 U.S. combat forces would remain in Afghanistan through the end of his presidency.

Has the USA's lack of success in Afghanistan proven similar to the Soviet failure there and inadvertently contributed to the rise of ISIS? Sadly, rather than exterminating the terrorists, Operation Enduring Freedom succeeded only in scattering them like roaches into caves and across borders, in turn enabling them to incubate and multiply in new breeding grounds like Pakistan and Syria, from whence ISIS made its fearsome debut. As for Afghanistan itself, it remains one of the poorest nations on earth, ranks as the world's fourth most corrupt country,[53] and what little freedom it enjoys exists only because of enduring foreign occupation.

IRAQ

In the summer of 2002, when U.S. President George W. Bush first began contemplating military action in Iraq, then-Secretary of State Colin Powell cautioned him about the ramifications of overthrowing the country's government. "You break it, you own it," said Powell,[54] who went on years later to elaborate on what had eventually been nicknamed the "Pottery Barn Rule."

"What I was saying is, if you get yourself involved—if you break a government, if you cause it to come down, by invading or other means, remember that you are now the government. You have a responsibility to take care of the people of that country."[55]

Mr. Bush understood Powell's analogy. The U.S. had invaded Afghanistan less than a month after the September 2001 attacks, but that country was already broken and the American military was essentially wading through the rubble to try and find Osama bin Laden. The President knew that invading Iraq would be different. Unlike Afghanistan, where the Taliban terrorized a largely defenseless populace under the pretense of civil authority, Iraq actually had a functioning government, albeit one presided over by the sadistic Saddam Hussein. In deposing Saddam, Secretary Powell was saying, America would have to occupy Iraq until some indigenous, stable government could take over. In other words, "owning" the nation meant rebuilding it. Still, Bush was optimistic that, with American guidance, a democratic Iraq could be built, and his administration set about to create a detailed path to success.

> We planned to prestation food, blankets, medicine, tents, and other relief supplies. We produced maps of where refugees could be sheltered. We deployed experienced humanitarian relief experts to enter Iraq alongside our troops. We had pinpointed the locations of most of Iraq's fifty-five thousand food distribution points and made arrangements with international organizations—including the World Food Programme—to make sure plenty of food was available.
>
> We also developed plans for long-term reconstruction. We focused on ten areas: education, health, water and sanitation, electricity, shelter, transportation, governance and rule of

> law, agriculture, communications, and economic policy. For each, we gathered data, formulated a strategy, and set precise goals....One of the toughest questions was how to plan for a post-Saddam political system. Some in the administration suggested that we turn over power immediately to a group of Iraqi exiles [but] I felt strongly that the Iraqis' first leader should be someone they selected. I was mindful of the British experience in Iraq in the 1920s. Great Britain had installed a non-Iraqi king, Faisal, who was viewed as illegitimate and whose appointment stoked resentment and instability. We were not going to repeat that mistake.[56]

An American-led coalition invaded Iraq on March 19, 2003, and 43 days later victory was declared. Then, on May 11, American diplomat Paul Bremer was appointed Administrator of the new Coalition Provisional Authority of Iraq. It was time to rebuild the nation.

In January 2005, free elections were held, and the sight of millions of Iraqi voters' uplifted index fingers dyed with indelible purple ink (to prevent double voting) appeared to vindicate President Bush's faith that a free and democratic Iraq could be established. Despite a threat from al Qaeda in Iraq to "wash the streets in blood," 58 percent of the Iraqi population voted in favor of a new National Assembly, chiefly comprised of members of the born-again nation's three leading political parties.

But appearances were deceiving. Voter turnout amongst Iraq's Sunni minority—who comprised some 15-20 percent of the population—was low, especially in Anbar province, where 98 percent of a distrusting electorate stayed home. As a result, the new National Assembly, although it had seated representatives from twelve different parties, was lopsidedly Shi'a Muslim.

In August, a new Iraqi Constitution was ratified, once again stoking the flame of liberty. But it is one thing to vote for freedom and another to maintain it. In the months following, only the Kurds of northern Iraq capitalized on their historic opportunity, to such an astonishing degree that the province quickly came to be known as the "Other Iraq." Meanwhile, the rest of the nation continued to struggle, as the Sunni minority in Anbar province actively resisted what they feared would be a Shi'a takeover.

The so-called American "surge" of 2007-'08 succeeded only after the Sunnis had been persuaded to join the new mainstream, and soon al Qaeda appeared to have been defeated once and for all. Finally, the prospect of a bright future appeared guaranteed, prompting President Bush and newly-elected Iraqi Prime Minister Nouri al-Maliki to sign a Status of Forces Agreement stating that all U.S. combat forces would vacate the nation by December 31, 2011.

But even as the strange and beautiful new atmosphere of peace settled over the nation, Prime Minister Maliki, whom many had long suspected of being a puppet of Shi'a-dominated Iran, began expunging Sunnis from positions of power, especially in the nation's military. In addition, he stopped paying the wages of rank-and-file Sunni officers and soldiers and withheld lawfully-budgeted provincial finances from Kurdistan, which for the time being flourished economically despite being shortchanged.

Maliki's alienation of the Sunnis and Kurds, combined with the gradual U.S. drawdown, created a vacuum in Iraq, even as Syria was beginning to catch fire next door. As a result, in June 2014, when ISIS crashed through the border from Syria into northern Iraq, the backdraft caused the whole region to explode. Here was the real "shock and awe," as a mere 800 ISIS fighters routed more than 30,000 Iraqi troops and police forces from the city nearly overnight. Many of the Shi'a soldiers shed their uniforms and fled the city in their underwear, while many Sunnis simply switched sides and joined the aggressors, who by now included key members of Saddam's old Baath Party, which had been outlawed and excluded from the new government in 2005.

It was a better outcome than ISIS leader Baghdadi could have dreamt of. Saddam's Baathist cronies, many of whom had served the dictator only for purposes of self-survival and personal gain, were nonetheless the nation's most experienced statesmen and military strategists. ISIS gave them a way to get revenge on Maliki and the Shi'a majority, as well as the Americans, who had purged them from the reconstituted Iraqi government in the first place.

President Obama, familiar with both Islam and the art of politics but a stranger to war, had only months earlier rejected Baghdadi and his evil clown show as counterfeit Muslims and hastily dismissed them militarily as a "jayvee squad." It was the same naïveté that Mr. Bush and other western leaders had earlier displayed: assessing the situation politically separately from the deeper cultural issue of ISIS' religious motivation. The result was a peculiar spectacle: secular Western politicians defining Islam as "a religion of peace" in the face of Muslim terrorists declaring that theirs "is the religion of the sword, not pacifism."[57]

This recurring blunder, just as in Afghanistan, bore tragic fruit in Iraq. Once again, a nation that had been supplied with the building blocks of democracy had failed to build one, because they lacked the cultural and spiritual foundation to do so.

But how do you rebuild a structure that, in the truest sense, never really existed in the first place? Yes, the Sykes-Picot agreement enacted in 1920 created a "State of Iraq" on paper, but that was not the same as creating a unified culture from disparate people groups. Nonetheless, Britain and France threw together Persian Shi'a, Arab Sunnis and

Kurds, purposely creating an unstable admixture that would "need" the help of its western benefactors for the foreseeable future.

That future never came, even after Iraq was granted legal independence in 1932. Instead there followed a series of coups and revolutions until Saddam Hussein assumed control in July 1979, just five months before the Ayatollah Khomeini took charge in Iran. For the next 24 years, fear of Saddam was the glue that held the fractured pieces together, along with occasional help from a self-interested West, as one U.S. President after another concluded that, in some cases, helping a madman makes strategic sense, because international politics, like nature, abhors a vacuum.

There is no reason to doubt that Mr. Bush, himself, harbored anything but good intentions when confronted with the world terror crisis that, on September 11, 2001, escalated to dizzying new heights. But good intentions are easily undermined by naïveté, and rarely has there been a more naïve notion than that of Muslim democracy, especially in the Arab world. Dissenters may point to non-Arab governments in places like Turkey, Indonesia, Malaysia and, more recently, Egypt, as examples of Muslim democracies. But each of those nations either directly represses non-Muslims or turns a governmental blind eye to their persecution by the popular majority.

This is not to say that a Muslim democracy with true freedom of religion cannot happen, but rather that it has not, and is in fact a contradiction in terms that can only be resolved by fundamental changes to Islam itself, as Ayaan Hirsi Ali suggests in her book, *Heretic: Why Islam Needs a Reformation Now.*

> I have identified five precepts central to the faith that have made it resistant to historical change and adaptation. Only when these five things are recognized as inherently

> harmful and when they are repudiated and nullified will a true Muslim Reformation have been achieved. The five things to be reformed are: 1. Muhammad's semi-divine and infallible status along with the literalist reading of the Qur'an, particularly those parts that were revealed in Medina; 2. The investment in life after death instead of life before death; 3. Shariah, the body of legislation derived from the Qur'an, the hadith, and the rest of Islamic jurisprudence; 4. The practice of empowering individuals to enforce Islamic law by commanding right and forbidding wrong; 5. The imperative to wage jihad, or holy war.[58]

Such a "reformation" is unimaginable, in that separating mosque and state would amount to deconstructing Islam, and in at least half a billion eyes would also constitute a complete repudiation of Muhammad himself, simply because the Prophet's Quranic model makes civil government a function of sword-bearing Muslim clergy, rendering politics nothing more than the outworking of religion. And that is precisely the model to which Abu Bakr al Baghdadi and ISIS are so fiercely dedicated.

At this writing, the Iraq drawn on world maps is a fiction. Mosul and the rest of the Nineveh Plain to the north, as well as large portions of Anbar province to the west, have been annexed by ISIS' caliphate. Kurdistan, to the north and east, soldiers bravely on, but with their economy now in shambles thanks to Maliki's treachery and a recent flood of refugees, they are beseeching America to help them, thus far to little avail. Centered in Baghdad to the south, the Iranian client state that still calls itself Iraq has given up on America and asked Russia to step in, a request that Russian President Vladimir Putin is happy to oblige.

It is time to ask the question again: *Did we cause ISIS?*

No. As Thomas Jefferson so accurately observed some 230 years ago, it was the violent brand of Islam that we now call *Islamism* that gave rise to the Barbary pirates, the ISIS of Jefferson's day. America's contribution to the current mess lies in the fact that several recent Presidents have either never read Jefferson's notes on the subject or have refused to acknowledge them.

Presidents George W. Bush and Barack Obama, for example, are diametrically opposed in their doctrines of foreign policy and war, yet neither seems willing to acknowledge Jefferson's insight that radical Islam—Islamism—views religion and politics as one in the same, as though doing so would be an indictment of Islam itself. This is the political equivalent of macular degeneration, the inability to see what is directly in one's path, and it is a blindness that affects not just American Presidents, but nearly every leader in the West. Thus afflicted, these leaders' good intentions have helped pave Iraq's road to ISIS hell.

SYRIA

As noted in Chapter 2, Phase Four of the "al Qaeda 20-Year Plan" proposed instigating, from 2010-13, the collapse of hated Arab governments. The stunning success of that phase, whether accomplished by al Qaeda, the Muslim Brotherhood, or some combination of players, was seen in the fall of governments in Egypt, Yemen, Tunisia, and Libya and the 2012 eruption of a full-scale civil war in Syria.

With Syrian President Bashar al-Assad's power seriously threatened by rebel forces, rumors began to circulate in Western intelligence circles that he was considering using chemical weapons, probably passed to him ten years earlier from Saddam Hussein, against his own people.

"We have been very clear to the Assad regime, but also to other players on the ground," said President Obama at a White House press briefing on August 20, 2012,[59] "that a red line for us is we start seeing a whole bunch of chemical weapons moving around or being utilized. That would change my calculus. That would change my equation."

Knowing that he needed to back his threat with action, the President ordered his military advisers to choose targets for a series of air strikes to begin on Friday, August 31, only to order them to stand down at the last minute. Instead of taking direct action, the President later explained, the United States would arm and assist Syrian rebels in fighting Assad, while pursuing the removal of chemical weapons from the country by diplomatic means. Those efforts failed, and one year later in August 2013, Bashar al-Assad did indeed use sarin gas to kill 1,400 Syrian men, woman and children in a rebel-held suburb of Damascus.

Meanwhile, future ISIS leader Baghdadi had immediately set about exploiting the President's decision not to attack by promising disappointed Syrian locals that his groups, al Qaeda in Iraq and the local al Nusra Front, would supply the protection that America had failed to provide. Then, in April 2013, he had merged the two groups into a new one called the Islamic State of Iraq and al-Sham (ISIS) and was already acquiring many of the arms the United States had promised to what President Obama called "moderate opposition" forces. This unintentional arming of the enemy would continue in 2014, as ISIS staged its virtually unopposed attack on Mosul.

Rather than focus its energy on officially overthrowing the Syrian government, ISIS has instead concentrated on acquiring territory for its caliphate, beginning with the establishment of its "capital" in Raqqa in northern Syria, and then expanding both southward into central Syria as well as annexing a large portion of northern Iraq.

DID WE CAUSE ISIS?

Neither President George W. Bush nor President Barack Obama directly "caused" ISIS anymore than Britain's Neville Chamberlain turned

Adolph Hitler from a reserve corporal into the killer of six million Jews. No, Abu Bakr al-Baghdadi created ISIS. Nevertheless, just as a 90-pound coed with a martial-arts black belt can subdue a large attacker by using his size against him, Baghdadi has often successfully leveraged both our action and inaction, whether appropriating military equipment supplied by the Bush administration or capitalizing on Obama's red-line failure in Syria.

The ISIS leader may be savage, but neither he nor his lieutenants are cavemen. One of them, in fact, has written a fiendishly intelligent terror handbook called "The Management of Savagery," whose methods ISIS has successfully employed to grow its wealth, ranks and territory. Elaborately staged and televised beheadings, for example, far from being displays of uncontrolled bloodlust, are purposeful tactics designed to melt enemy resistance, paving the way for easier territorial gains in the future.

Also, unlike al Qaeda or the Shi'a leaders of Iran, who seem to find their identity in destruction, Baghdadi seeks above all to build the caliphate. In his mind, the annihilation of America and her allies is but a prophetic stepping stone to that goal. The U.S. failed to understand this, falsely assuming that ISIS was simply a more brutish incarnation of al Qaeda, and therefore more primitive. Thus, whenever ISIS' advances have been stymied, the West has naïvely assumed they were in retreat. In reality, Baghdadi uses the pauses in fighting in order to consolidate power in territory he already controls, while using the beheadings, etc., to maintain high levels of fear and publicity.

No, America did not create ISIS, but her political lurching to the right and left—with allies often following in tow—have somehow paved a center path that indeed helped contribute to the formation, strengthening and enrichment of ISIS, a foe with far more masterful skills than anyone anticipated.

At this writing, more than 4 million Syrians have fled their homeland, and Russian President Vladimir Putin has exploited America's absence in Syria and Iraq to begin reestablishing his nation's military influence on the world stage. And what better theater than the oil-rich Middle East? Russia, already one of the world's major oil suppliers, could use newfound influence there to retaliate against the U.S. and the European Union economic sanctions imposed after Moscow's 2014 invasion of Ukraine and subsequent annexation of the Crimea.

So, what can America do? This subject will be fully addressed in Chapters 10 and 11. But, one immediate lesson to be learned from the debacles in Syria and Iraq is that leaving weapons, vehicles and other munitions in undependable hands is ultimately more expensive than bringing them home. It would be wiser that they be removed or completely destroyed, down to the last spare tire.

A second lesson concerns covert operations to try and find ISIS feeder roots, especially with regard to the group's funding. Thankfully, this is one area in which the U.S. has been active, as evidenced by a recent airstrike in Mosul that destroyed a $145 million stockpile of ISIS cash. At last, former Secretary Powell's Pottery Barn Rule begins to work in our favor: Destroying ISIS' finances would go a long way towards stopping them in their tracks, and keep them from conducting their "management of savagery" elsewhere.

7

BLOOD MONEY

"For the love of money is a root of all kinds of evil."

ST. PAUL

If you've ever wondered where ISIS gets its money, you could start in Syria's oil fields, the plundered ruins of Palmyra, the looted banks of Iraq, a few deep pockets in Kuwait, Qatar and Saudi Arabia, or the emptied accounts of ransom-paying Europeans.

Unfortunately, you could also start at the U.S. Department of Defense in Washington, D.C.

Neither President Barack Obama nor his best experts could have imagined the calamitous consequences that unfolded in the Middle East from 2011 to 2014, as an ostensible rebel fighting force in Syria used cash, training and arms supplied by the American military to transform itself into ISIS. On an official basis, the U.S. was training a group of Syrian military defectors called the Free Syrian Army to fight against dictator Bashar al-Assad, but infighting amongst factions within that group helped undermine it from its 2011 inception. Seeing an opportunity, Abu Bakr al-Baghdadi first formed a Syrian branch of al Qaeda in

Iraq, called the al Nusra Front, and then later merged the two groups into ISIS, a force whose discipline and ferocity enticed a large number of Free Syrian Army officers and soldiers to defect yet again.

ISIS' first big payday at U.S. expense came with their 2014 invasion of Mosul, as 30,000 Iraqi troops and security officers fled before less than a thousand ISIS fighters. Within days, news networks around the world ran footage of U.S. Army Humvees and tanks flying the black flag of the Islamic State. It took eleven months to calculate the totals of American-made weaponry that had fallen into ISIS' hands during the Mosul conquest, but finally, in June 2015, new Iraqi Prime Minister Haider al-Abadi released the first detailed accounting: 2,300 Humvee armored vehicles, 40 M1A1 Abram tanks, 52 M198 Howitzer mobile gun systems and 74,000 Army machine guns. The total value, as estimated by thefiscaltimes.com, exceeded $650 million, instantly making ISIS the wealthiest terror group in history. Yet, "experts say those losses represent just a portion of the many hundreds of millions of dollars' worth of U.S.-supplied military equipment that has fallen into ISIS' hands and is being used against the U.S. and allied forces on the ground in Iraq and neighboring Syria."[60]

PLUNDERING THE PAST

ISIS' is equally adept at turning salvaged material into hard cash, and smart enough to cover their financial tracks in layers of debris. For example, during the siege of Mosul, the group bombed *al-Nabi Yunus*, the tomb of the biblical prophet, Jonah, just east of the Tigris River on the site of ancient Nineveh, but only after looting its contents for later sale. Over the nearly three millennia since his death, the legendary Old Testament prophet's grave had been built up, first into an Assyrian tomb, then a hilltop Christian church and finally, in the 14th Century, an ornate Muslim shrine, decorated with Persian carpets of woven silk and silver, copper candlesticks, ornate hanging ostrich eggshells and other adornments. For more than 2,700 years, it had survived nearly a dozen conquests by the likes of Cyrus, King of the Medes and Persians, Alexander the Great, Saladin, the Mongol Hordes, Suleiman, the Allies of World War I and, most recently, the U.S. Army.

Sadly all of the shrine's historical and cultural glory disintegrated in a single moment in late July 2014, when ISIS plundered its treasures, lined it with explosives and blew it into a cloud of brown dirt. Not content with a single desecration, the terror group that same month also despoiled and destroyed the purported tombs of the Prophet Daniel, the Roman martyr St. George, and several more sites revered by Muslims and Christians alike, on the grounds that the Prophet Muhammad forbade "the plastering over of graves," as well as inscriptions and other markings thereon.

Usually lost on news crews preoccupied with the big explosions is the fact that ISIS' dynamite and sledgehammers are only used on antiquities too big for transport, while smaller items such as coins and ancient scrolls are sold on black markets in Turkish bazaars, or laundered several times until they wind up in high-brow auctions in London and New York. Such piracy has netted ISIS at least $100 million as of September 2015.

Archeologist Joanne Farchakh described the money trail in an interview with Britain's *The Independent*. "First, ISIS sells the statues, stone faces and frescoes that international dealers demand," she said. "It takes the money, hands over the relics – and blows up the temples and buildings they come from to conceal the evidence of what has been looted."[61]

Sometimes the thieves are not members of ISIS, but unemployed Syrians, desperate to feed their own families and thus willing to appease their terrorist occupiers with up to half of the proceeds. Former CBS correspondent Clarissa Ward and her field producer, posing as buyers in Istanbul, were offered one such item: a 2,000-year old Roman Mosaic, potentially worth $100,000, that had been unearthed by locals in Syria.[62] Ironically, ISIS' share of the take from such sales buys the bombs and bullets that kill more Syrians.

A much more lucrative ISIS pursuit has been Iraqi banks. When the group's fighters invaded Mosul, a city of two million inhabitants, they met with no resistance, leaving more than 90 local banks ripe for the robbing. Initial reports that the terrorists had made off with some $429 million were quickly denied by officials in Baghdad, but one year later U.S. Treasury Assistant Secretary for Terror Financing, Daniel Glaser, not only reasserted those claims, but put the figure between $500 million and $1 billion.[63]

RANSOM AND HUMAN TRAFFICKING

Captured weapons, stolen antiquities and robbed banks provide quick cash, but are also exhaustible supplies, and Baghdadi knows this. That is why his Islamic State also monetizes a renewable resource called humanity. Kidnapping, extortion, taxation and the outright buying and selling of women and children in public auctions is a thriving business for the caliphate that aims to redeem mankind by enslaving it.

As with their slickly produced execution videos, ISIS has turned kidnapping into a sick art that makes millions. In 2014 alone, ransom brought the group more than $20 million, according to the U.S. Treasury Department.[64] However, a U.N. terrorism expert put the figure much higher, at $35-45 million,[65] an amount more in line with other estimates.

American journalist James Foley's beheading, the first in a grim series, was carried out as supposed retribution against America. "You have plotted against us and gone far out of your way to find reasons to interfere in our affairs," said Foley's British executioner. In reality, the journalist was killed only after a series of threatening emails to his parents and employer had failed to produce the $132 million ransom ISIS had demanded for his release.[66] The U.S. government also reportedly rejected a secret demand of $100 million, consistent with policy that prohibits paying such ransoms in order to discourage more kidnappings in the future.

Ignoring that reasoning, some European governments regularly accede to such demands, with the predictable result that more victims are kidnapped and for higher ransom amounts. France, for example, is thought to have paid $14 million for the release of four journalists,[67] a huge escalation from the average of $200,000 paid per victim in 2003.[68] In early 2015, two Italian aid workers were released by their captors in Syria in exchange for a reported $13 million. The Italian government denied that any money had been paid. But such denials are commonplace, and payments are often disguised, as when the German government paid some $5.5 million to free 32 hostages being held in the poverty-stricken African nation of Mali, while officially earmarking the money as humanitarian aid.[69]

The caliphate's rulers are also not above kidnapping their own "citizens" when they need a quick infusion of cash. According to Atheel al-Nujaifi, the former governor of Iraq's Nineveh province, ISIS will demand anywhere from $500 to $200,000, with some families going so far as to sell their farms and livestock in order to rescue a loved one.[70]

Prices are even lower in slave markets, where non-Muslims and foreign captives are not held as dear, and where ISIS' most perverse motivations are revealed: The smallest children bring the highest price.

"For Islamic State fighters, the prices in Iraqi dinars for boys and girls aged 1 to 9 are equal to about $165, [senior U.N. official Zainab] Bangura said. Prices for adolescent girls are $124 and it's less for women over 20....The girls get peddled like barrels of petrol....One girl can be sold and bought by five or six different men. Sometimes these fighters sell the girls back to their families for thousands of dollars of ransom."[71]

Women over 50 are not even listed as for sale, a likely indicator that, holding no value, they are killed and discarded as trash. Such a fate would be consistent with other treatment, such as their 2015 Ramadan holiday contest, in which ISIS fighters were encouraged to memorize the Qur'an's most warlike passages, with the top three winners each receiving a female slave captured in war. "We ask the great lord to make your life easier and to grant you with what he loves and what pleases him," said a poster announcing the contest.

TAXES AND CONFISCATION

In addition to extortion and kidnapping, ISIS levies heavy taxes and, perhaps most profitably of all, simply confiscates properties. Combined, these four sources net the group enough income to run day-to-day operations internally. In fact, according to what appears to be leaked ISIS records, subsequently published by terror watchdog Aaron Y. Zelin on his website, jihadology.net, the group's income from "confiscations" in December 2014 amounted to 44.7% of their total income, with oil and gas at 27.7% and taxes close behind at 23.7%.[72]

If these percentages indicate an overall shift, they represent an enormous boon to ISIS, since not requiring external funding makes it much easier for them to cover their financial tracks, in turn making them harder to fight. It also makes governing easier, since, unlike oil fields, practices cannot be bombed. And for many of the millions who suffer under their rule, eking out a daily existence under the threat of war is at least an improvement over living through one.

"Despite all this, there are many people in Raqqa who are happy that some semblance of life has returned, and they accept these payments as a tax," says journalist-turned-author Benjamin Hall. "Raqqa's central bank is now the ISIS tax authority, where every two months shop owners come and pay twenty dollars for electricity, water, and security. They're happy as long as they see it as a better life than the chaos of war— it remains to be seen how long they can put up with the brutality though."[73]

ISIS also extorts its immediate neighbors, especially within Syria, where they sell both electricity and oil to Bashar al-Assad's government, which consents to pay them, considering that, until recently, Assad had become too weak to take back the infrastructure the group had seized. In fact, as of early September 2015, ISIS had either captured or was close to capturing, the last of Syria's oil fields.[74]

In Iraq, Baghdadi's group had been extorting banks and businesses in Mosul and the Nineveh Plain for at least several months before their 2014 summer siege of that territory. According to the online news network *Agence France Presse* and reported by Breitbart[75], ISIS had been collecting $5 million per month before the invasion, an amount that more than doubled to $11 million per month afterward.

Taxation in the caliphate amounts to extortion billed by the month, and is so oppressive that many businesses have been forced to close, while those that remain have had to raise prices by as much as 1,000% just to cope. As in the old Soviet Union, only the privileged—in this case ISIS fighters—can afford meat and chicken, while everyone else subsists on basic vegetables such as cucumbers, tomatoes and potatoes.

More than a matter of cruelty, such oppression and suffocating tax rates are likely part of a strategy to push residents into joining ISIS. According to the Atlantic,[76] the tactic appears to be working: in Palmyra alone, more than 1,000 young men had joined ISIS within the first five months after that city's capture in May 2015.

BLACK GOLD

In early September 2015, ISIS fighters attacked Jazal, an oil field a few miles west of Palmyra, Syria. The fact that this was the last Syrian field not already under the group's control may have made the assault the last straw that caused the nation's besieged President, Bashar al-Assad, to welcome Russian jets and tanks into his country a week later.

At one point in 2014, ISIS' income from captured oil fields in Syria and Iraq had reached an estimated $3 million per day, an amount so alarmingly high that the U.S. Government felt compelled to begin air attacks. At this writing, the ongoing sorties have cut the group's oil revenues by at least two-thirds, and perhaps even more severely if the leaked papers at the usually reliable jihadology.net are to be believed.[77]

Whatever the truth, it is clear that even with reduced prices ISIS continues, in part, to finance its reign of terror by capturing Iraqi and Syrian oil and then selling it on the black market to neighboring governments. So reliant are these countries that even the Iraqi Kurds, ISIS' fiercest opponents, reportedly have occasionally been forced to buy crude from the group.

It is also possible that the lower gasoline prices U.S. drivers have enjoyed in recent times are part of a double-barreled strategy by the Saudis and other Middle East oil producers, not only to curb the profitability of "fracking" by their American competition, but also to make oil a less lucrative commodity for ISIS to peddle on black markets.

FOREIGN FUNDS

When Syria's civil war broke out in 2011, it was not only the U.S. that decided to support rebels fighting the brutal Assad regime. Various regional governments and private channels also eagerly chipped in, not only because most were Sunnis eager to rid the world of a Shi'a dictator—Assad is an Alawite, a controversial subsect of the Shi'a—but also because it was a convenient way to hide their support for various jihadist groups vying for power in the conflict.

In 2013, under pressure from the U.S., Saudi Arabia passed a law criminalizing support to any terrorist organization, but even with that restriction ISIS was able to take in about $40 million from various Persian Gulf sources, including government members and royalty.[78] Qatar and Kuwait, in particular, lack careful monitoring of their banking systems. This makes funneling money relatively easy in both countries, with the funds often vaguely marked as "humanitarian aid." Additionally, the use of social media—especially popular texting apps that include geo-location—helps terror sponsors coordinate drop-off points that can be changed up to the last minute before delivery. The fact that western app makers are especially concerned about being accused of surveilling their customers facilitates the process even more.

Ironically, the Kuwaiti government, which used to turn a blind eye to Sunni clerics who raised large sums for ISIS-linked groups, now fears that it is ripe for attack, as evidence by its October 2015 $2.8 billion defense deal with France. Other nations, such as Egypt, Qatar, United Arab Emirates and Saudi Arabia have also turned to the French, not only for military supplies but also training.

THE BOTTOM LINE

While ISIS' oil revenues have been interrupted by the West's air campaign, they still are storing much of their financial haul within the territories they call their caliphate, with total annual income estimated most recently at more than $900 million. If there is a financial Achilles' heel for the group, it is that they survive like locusts, consuming everything and everyone in their path until eventually nothing remains. Even for themselves. Since the establishment of their caliphate in the summer of 2014, they have ravaged more than 4,000 historic sites in Syria, rifled the wealth of most business owners, lost countless others to the exodus of refugees fleeing into Europe, taxed their hostage population to the point of starvation and captured oil fields that they can temporarily operate but not permanently maintain. In the language of war, ISIS is committing scorched earth against its own caliphate.

It is possible that both Russia and Iran know this, and have been waiting on the sidelines until they could step in and overcome a weakened Islamic State, thus becoming the heroes and seizing stature from the U.S. on the world stage. But of course, Vladimir Putin's Russia, more than ever, is Winston Churchill's "riddle, wrapped in a mystery, inside an enigma." Predicting what the Russian strongman might do, especially when faced with a more isolationist America, is a very difficult task. And the fact that Iran has lately been engaged in hand-holding with Russia makes a post-ISIS world seem an even more dangerous place.

8

IS THIS WORLD WAR III?

"I believe it is peace for our time...
Go home and get a nice quiet sleep."

NEVILLE CHAMBERLAIN, 1938

After ISIS bombed a passenger-packed Russian airliner in October 2015, killing 224 passengers and crew, and then only days later massacred more than 120 persons in Paris, Pope Francis and the leaders of France, Israel and Jordan all declared aloud what until then had been a reluctant whisper: for the third time in 100 years, they said, the world was at war. Other heads of state, most notably U.S. President Obama, demurred, knowing that such a pronouncement would be tantamount to a declaration of war, and could possibly trigger the formation of alliances that would once again pit the U.S. and Russia squarely against one another.

So, what is the truth? Is America officially denying a world war that, although it lacks a Roman numeral, has already begun? Or has ISIS been contained, as some government officials insist, as part of a strategy designed to starve it of resources until it eventually collapses?

The truth is simpler than either question presupposes: ISIS has declared war on the world, so the world is at war. This time, however, the conflict is an asymmetrical one without measurable front lines. Thus, despite ISIS' geographical caliphate, its army cannot simply be "contained," as attacks from San Bernardino to Burkina Faso attest. Western declarations aside, therefore, the hour has come for lovers of peace everywhere to sharpen their senses, prepare their minds and adjust their lifestyles. A new Hitler has arrived, but this one is not a man. It is a cancer of the soul that has spread, black and vine-like, through the spiritual fiber of the Arab world, and is seeking new nodes to infect, especially in the hated West.

ALL THE WORLD'S A STAGE

Barack Obama's 2008 campaign for the presidency was so stunningly successful that he was awarded the Nobel Peace Prize even before taking office, based on his multicultural ideals, humble acknowledgment of America's past shortcomings and his promise to bring about "fundamental transformation." Once in office, the new President kept his word, embracing a somewhat dovish foreign policy heavily reliant on the late Nelson Mandela's philosophy that "it is better to lead from behind and to put others in front."

War, however, has a way of turning doves into sitting ducks. Six and a half years and a spate of ISIS terror attacks into his presidency, President Obama found himself the target of previously friendly American media outlets and political allies, who now were criticizing the very qualities for which they once had praised him.

"The war against [ISIS] requires the kind of leadership that has gone missing," said the dateline of *TIME* magazine's November 30, 2015 cover story, after the President had given a tepid response to a week of terror attacks in Lebanon, France, and Mali. "Facing the press at an international summit in Turkey, he was weary and querulous when the world wanted galvanizing," the magazine complained.[79]

"An effective response will require the Obama Administration to be out in front: there must be no leading from behind in this effort," wrote the Council on Foreign Relations' Stewart M. Patrick in an opinion piece for *Newsweek*.[80]

"ISIL is not contained. ISIL is expanding," said California's Democrat Senator Dianne Feinstein, directly contradicting the President in a television interview with MSNBC. "I've never been more concerned."[81]

History will judge whether Mr. Obama's policies are rooted in altruism or demonstrate a lack of leadership. To be sure, he inherited a truckload of problems, but his sharp ideological left turn may have wrecked the truck. Whatever the case, rogue states like Iran, opportunists like Russia's Putin, as well as France and the Kurds of Iraq, both of whom ISIS has attacked on their home soil, have decided against waiting for history's verdict. They see a self-proclaimed state that has managed to take enough territory and control enough resources to function like one, and have decided to act against it, with or without the U.S. Adding to the mix is a tinderbox of unstable Sunni Muslim states whose populations, three-fifths of them under the age of 30,[82] are fed up on the one hand with wealthy plutocrats whom they see as concubines of the West, and on the other are seething with hatred towards Shi'a-dominated Iran, whose appetite for a new Persian empire poses as big an existential threat to them as ISIS.

Given such instability, it is necessary to look at some of the main players in what *TIME* magazine has called "World War ISIS,"[83] in order to properly assess and prepare for what the near future holds, whether it be war or peace. A natural starting point is found in the most unstable state of all: Syria.

SYRIA

As noted previously, the world of Islam has long been divided between two main sects: the Sunnis, who constitute nearly four-fifths of the world's 1.6 billion Muslim population, and the Shi'a, a more mystical minority numbering upwards of 200 million adherents, who predominate in Iran, Iraq, Azerbaijan and Bahrain, and who claim small but significant minorities in Saudi Arabia, India and several other countries. Given the historical animosity between the two groups, it should not be surprising that some of the most savage repression in the Arab world has taken place In Iraq and Syria, where for so long the minority ruled. In Iraq, it was strongman Saddam Hussein, a Sunni-born political secularist, who brutalized the Shi'a majority for a quarter century. In Syria, an opposite arrangement made for the same result, as an overwhelmingly Sunni population suffered under the Shi'a dictators Hafez al-Assad, who ruled from 1970 until his death in 2000, and his successor son, Bashar al-Assad.

Having come to power in 2000, the younger Assad had witnessed Saddam's downfall in Iraq just three years later, and then had watched subsequent regional unrest culminate in revolutions in Tunisia, Egypt, Libya and Yemen from 2010-2012. Thus, when the the Syrian uprising began in 2011, Assad was more than happy to call upon Iran, whose 36 years of governmental stability and civil order made it an attractive protector until the embattled dictator could call on someone more formidable.

IRAN

Virtually surrounded and vastly outnumbered by regional enemies after its own Islamic Revolution in 1979, Iran had been forced to build and maintain an efficient military machine that served it well in quelling both a Kurdish rebellion and surviving an eight year war with neighboring Iraq. Additionally, the Iranians already had their fingers in a dozen political pots around the world, including nearby Lebanon, and Assad knew that they would welcome an invitation to further strengthen their influence in the region.

As for Iran's Grand Ayatollah Ali Khamenei, who has ruled in Tehran since his predecessor's death in 1989, establishing a foothold in Syria would reinforce the west flank of the so-called Shi'a Crescent, a sickle-shaped swath of Shi'a-dominated territory that stretches from Bahrain in the south, northward through Iran and then westward through southern Iraq and out to the Mediterranean Sea. Khamenei, more than anyone else, holds the handle of this demographic sickle because it is critical to his power, and ultimately to Shi'a survival, in that it bisects an otherwise Sunni-dominated Middle East.

Protecting the Crescent from ISIS, not personal loyalty, was why the Ayatollah cooperated with Assad in reaching out to Russia. In July 2015, Khamenei defied a United Nations travel ban and dispatched the commander of his Revolutionary Guard and elite Quds Force, General Qasem Soleimani, to Moscow, at Vladimir Putin's request. Once Soleimani had delivered Assad's formal invitation for Russia to intervene in Syria militarily, his job was to join with Russian generals in hammering out the details.

ENTER RUSSIA

That ISIS is waging a religious war in Syria is most plainly evident in the "Alawite dog" epithet commonly hurled at President Assad and his closest advisors. Assad is a member of the Alawite sect, an offshoot of "Twelver" Shi'ism. Alawites number less than 3 million worldwide, with more than half of them provincially cushioned against the Mediterranean coastline in northern Syria. It is this religiously concentrated area to which Assad's best hopes for survival are attached, thanks especially to a midsize coastal city called Tartus.

"I think it's fair to say that many people believe Assad at this stage is trying to carve out a rump state for himself and the Alawites," a senior network news correspondent[84] who spent five years in Syria recently told the authors, "and that's what the Russians are currently helping him with."

As with Iran's Khamenei, what motivates Russian President Vladimir Putin is not compassion for Assad and his Alawite brethren, but his own interests. In this case, Putin is determined to protect Russia's naval base at Tartus, his country's only military presence on the Mediterranean coast. And Tartus lies in the heart of Assad's cherished Alawite enclave.

But a "rump state" is not enough for a dictator who grew up in grander surroundings. Emboldened by the fact that Russia needs him, at least for the time being, Assad is, at this writing, attempting to retake the northern city of Aleppo, once Syria's largest but now a bombed out shell that has seen 85 percent of its 2.1 million residents either die or flee northward to the nearby border with Turkey.

ISIS' downing of the Russian airliner gave Putin a pretext for expanding his sham air campaign against ISIS into a full-fledged Russian military presence on Syrian soil. Of course, destroying the terrorists' caliphate and liberating the country's suffering masses is not Putin's goal. Indeed, the vast majority of Russia's air strikes have not been targeted at ISIS at all, but have been indiscriminately dropped on civilians, especially in the now devastated cities of Homs and Aleppo. Instead, along with preserving Russia's naval base at Tartus, Putin likely sees other compelling reasons to establish a permanent foothold in Syria, first and foremost among them being the weakening of U.S. influence in the region.

Second, Iran's post-sanctions reentry into the world's economy brings with it petroleum reserves that are twice the size of Russia's reserves, and with plummeting oil prices already hammering the Russian economy, Mr. Putin has much to gain by lending a hand to both Iran and Syria in protecting Khamenei's "Shi'a Crescent." The benefits? For one thing, Putin has already called for a Eurasian currency union that would include Kazakhstan, whose southern border touches the Caspian seacoast a mere 300 miles north of Tehran, because he knows currencies equal clout. By establishing linkage of any kind between Russian and Iranian oil interests, Putin would gain further financial influence, and would be able to cast the Russian bear's shadow across other oil-producing nations, all the way to the Persian Gulf.

Third, by making the Syrian nightmare even more horrid via his wanton bombing of civilian centers, Putin can rest assured that additional tens of thousands of Syrians will seek refuge in Europe where, whether they are accepted or rejected, an already shaken European Union will face further destabilization.

Finally, the United States' foreign policy of "leading from behind" gives Putin a chance to turn Syria's civil war into his personal parade, and to play the hero if he actually decides to lead the charge in attacking ISIS' capital city of Raqqa. Russia may not yet have recovered its superpower status, but it is certainly willing to fill the vacuum left by one. And Putin has already set the stage for such mock heroics by blaming the U.S. for helping to create ISIS in the first place when it supplied arms to Syrian rebels fighting against Assad.

LIBYA

Syria is ISIS' main stage, of course, but the American-led coalition air strikes, combined with Russian support for Syrian President Assad in his efforts to regain lost territory, have curtailed the terror group's effectiveness and hurt their finances. Adding to the pressure, Turkey has made it difficult for the group to move new fighters across the border to replenish their ranks, with some intelligence reports reducing their highest estimates of ISIS fighters in Syria from 31,500 down to 25,000. As a result, Baghdadi has done what he always does when the hammer comes down: he makes his enemies play whack-a-mole, in this case diverting new recruits to the up-for-grabs North African nation of Libya.

Most Americans, if they are familiar with Libya at all, know it as the location of Benghazi, the northern coastal city where U.S. Ambassador Christopher Stevens and three other Americans were killed by Islamist militants in 2012. But Libya is more dangerous to the world than that. It is a country in chaos, a headless state where two rival governments and several rogue military factions have vied for power ever since October 2011, when a rebel mob beat to death strongman Muammar Gaddafi, who had ruled Libya for 42 years. With a land mass larger than Iran, but at 6.2 million people less than a tenth of Iran's population, Libya makes an ideal training ground for a group like ISIS. Additionally, with its hundreds of miles of unguarded Mediterranean seacoast to the north, and porous borders with Tunisia, Algeria, Chad, Niger, Sudan and Egypt, Libya is an ideal place from which to export terror as well.

It should be no surprise then, that ISIS leader Baghdadi has diverted thousands of new recruits to Libya, swelling their ranks from 3,000 ISIS fighters to at least 6,500 as of early 2016. He has already declared three ISIS *wilâyats* (provinces) there, including one that encompasses Libya's capital, Tripoli, and is no doubt eager to annex the entire nation to his caliphate. In fact, one report from December 2015 claims that Baghdadi is living in Libya, where he is purportedly recovering from injuries sustained two months prior when the Iraqi air force bombed his convoy in Iraq's Western Anbar province.[85]

In early February 2016, Defense Secretary Ashton B. Carter and Gen. Joseph F. Dunford Jr., the chairman of the Joint Chiefs of Staff, among others, called for either an American or allied ground force in Libya, but President Obama, wary of becoming entangled in yet another Muslim country, has thus far refused to make such a commitment.

MEANWHILE, BACK AT THE CALIPHATE...

If ISIS leader Baghdadi believes his own apocalyptic message, then his survival in the convoy bombing was reassurance from above. Likewise, his philosophy dictates that Iran's presence in Syria only hastens a forthcoming Shi'a body count. Exterminating the Shi'a is paramount to the caliph, since hatred for them is the lifeblood of every ISIS fighter's willingness to serve. "For all his savagery, Saddam did not make it a matter of state policy to seek the wholesale destruction of the Shi'a," write Michael Weiss and Hassan Hassan, explaining that "they were still tolerated in the upper echelons of the Iraqi military and in the Baath Party, even after the 1991 massacres. Al-Baghdadi, however, has so far demonstrated nothing short of annihilationist intention, following in the dark pathological tradition of [his predecessor] al-Zarqawi. To ISIS, the Shi'a are religiously void, deceitful, and only marked for death."[86]

The 2015 arrival of Russian bombers over the caliphate marked yet another milestone in Stage 6 of ISIS' 20-Year Plan, the period of "total confrontation." But Iran and Russia do not constitute nearly enough players to convene the apocalyptic war that must culminate at Dabiq sometime before the year 2020. Hence, ISIS' various attacks in such diverse places as France, California, Tunisia, Libya, Turkey and Indonesia, to name a few of the latest. In effect, the ISIS leader is doing his utmost to get as many plates spinning as he can before he crashes them all on purpose.

For their parts, France and Turkey have entered the fray. This is bound to please Baghdadi, who also delights when Vladimir Putin mocks his American counterpart, Russia provokes the Turks, Turkish jets bomb their own Kurds, refugees overwhelm their European hosts from Serbia to Sweden, and anti-immigrant protesters take to the streets of Warsaw, Prague, Dresden, Calais and Amsterdam. His end-of-days vision is likewise affirmed when Bashar al-Assad's barrel bombs make instant martyrs of ISIS soldiers defending their hold on Aleppo. None of this is too much for a man who, in August 2014, publicized the inauguration of his Islamist paradise with a video of 200 children forced to lie face down in the dirt, side by side, and then machine-gunned to pieces by the "faithful."

Why is Baghdadi so unbelievably savage? Because the gateway to jihadist heaven must be laden with guns, chemicals, explosions, stacks of bodies and pink sludge that used to be bodies. And the only way to pile the bloody bounty high enough to please his god is to provoke the Great Satan himself—the United States of America—to join the war that Baghdadi believes will bring back the Mahdi, Islam's savior (who is sometimes rumored to be Baghdadi himself). Then the Mahdi—remember, this must take place before 2020—will lead ISIS' black-robed brigade forward to blot out the present world, and make room for the prophet Jesus to return and usher in the gluttonous, orgiastic Paradise of jihadist dreams, where the wine overflows, the tables are always full, slaves are eager to be owned, and where innumerable virgins long to be ravished as frequently as possible.

It is this black cancer of the soul that has crept across the Arab world, metastasizing in the minds of young men who have been raised in a marinade of hate. The same cancer now penetrates the West, wrapping itself around the minds and hearts of purposeless youth who have grown up feeding on the dry husks of secularism, and who crave something—anything—that will fill their inner void, even if it kills them.

WAR OF THE WORLDS

The 2005 movie remake of H.G. Wells' *War of the Worlds* featured alien invaders in giant, three-legged war machines, bursting up from beneath the ground to scoop up humans by the millions to feast upon their blood. Throughout the film the aliens seem unstoppable, with mankind's mightiest bombs and missiles failing to halt a single step as the massive tripods carry them across the earth. Yet, the story's end finds the tripods collapsing and the aliens dying in agony. They were doomed from the start, the viewer learns, by the smallest of earth's inhabitants: disease-carrying bacteria to which humans are immune.

Like H.G. Wells' invaders, ISIS has appeared unstoppable at times, a monstrous machine with a thirst for blood so foreign to humanity as to appear to have burst up from Hell itself. Yet, just as with monsters in the movies, this one is not indestructible. For behind its outer shell there are small creatures, two-legged *things* who have made themselves so subhuman that they cannot survive in a world made for man. ISIS is doomed.

Unlike the movie narrative, however, it is not nature that will send the terrorists back to hell from whence they came, but wisdom, courage, and—most important—a true uniting of wills.

Thus far, ISIS owes a great deal of its success to the backstabbing and hypocrisy of a rogue's gallery of Arab governments and oligarchs who have allowed Baghdadi and company to do their dirty work for them, destabilizing rival governments, destroying competing industries, killing off Shi'a and other irksome minorities and simply stealing Syria's oil, which ISIS often sells on the cheap to governments who claim to oppose them. Even Syria's Assad has purchased oil from the terrorists who have vowed to bring him down.

With such intrigue behind the scenes in the Middle East and so much reluctance in the West, the question becomes: Who does have the spirit to be the first to take on Baghdadi and his black-clad demons?

The answer is that victory over the caliphate that is not a caliphate, is a nation that is not a nation.

9

FROM DARKNESS TO DAWN

"Tell America we will be your boots on the ground. We can defeat ISIS."

THE HONORABLE KARIM SINJARI, INTERIOR MINISTER, IRAQI KURDISTAN

It is easy to look at the simmering mess that has long been the Middle East and conclude that ISIS has sealed its fate as an unquenchable Lake of Fire, and to hope and pray that ISIS leader Baghdadi and his minions will somehow gnaw one another to death before they can eat too many holes in the West. But there is no good reason to cede the historic momentum to them. In reality, ISIS is a relatively small but fierce enemy that might well have been prevented from arising in the first place, had the Obama administration taken seriously the warnings of their own Defense Intelligence Agency back in 2011-2012.

One DIA report, issued August 5, 2012 and declassified in 2015 following a successful lawsuit by the conservative watchdog Judicial Watch, warned that, "If the situation unravels [in Syria] there is the possibility of establishing a declared or undeclared salafist principality in eastern Syria (Hasaka and Der Zor), and this is exactly what the supporting powers to the opposition want, in order to isolate the Syrian regime." Continued lax security, it cautioned, "creates the ideal atmosphere for AQI (Al Qaeda in Iraq) to return to its old pockets in Mosul and Ramadi," and that "ISI [Islamic State of Iraq] could also declare an Islamic state through its union with other terrorist organizations in Iraq and Syria, which will create grave danger in regards to unifying Iraq and the protection of its territory."[87]

Whether or not President Obama was personally briefed on the DIA report is unknown, but it was circulated to the CIA and State Department as well as other senior leaders who normally report to the President. The fact remains, however, that ISI did indeed declare its Islamic State (ISIS) in April 2013, and that the President dismissed them as a "jayvee squad" a full seventeen months after the DIA warning.

What is clear is that Mr. Obama had originally begun quietly arming Syrian rebels in mid-2012 in hopes that they would remove the country's dictator, Bashar al-Assad, in a technically secret move that was reported first by the Reuters news service in early August of that year and quickly confirmed to CNN.[88]

"Providing sophisticated weaponry to the rebels may aid their cause, but it also could assist America's enemies," warned the Washington *Times*, noting that, "The State Department recently confirmed that al Qaeda fighters are moving into Syria from Iraq and elsewhere, and the terror group will seek to exploit the chaos, as it has done with the Arab Spring violence."[89]

HOUSE DIVIDED

The *Times* criticism proved to be an understated prophecy. Just as with President George H.W. Bush's failure to deal decisively with Saddam Hussein in the 1991 Gulf war, and the younger President Bush's attempt at nation building after removing Saddam, President Obama's move to arm the Syrian opposition fell victim to the only law that seems to apply unfailingly in the Arab world: the law of unintended consequences. In other words, America "got played"...again.

Less than a year after U.S. arms began flowing into Syria, ISIS declared itself a "state," an action dismissed as symbolic and of little consequence at first, but one that instead proved to be a brilliant recruitment tool. And then, within two years, a much larger ISIS force invaded northern Iraq and declared a caliphate. Now they had land, the primary ingredient of an actual state.

But while the group's capture of physical territory was a startling success, ISIS proved equally adept at captivating minds and terrorizing hearts. Always seemingly a step ahead of their opponents, ISIS' media department eventually began churning out some 200,000 recruitment posts and threatening tweets every day, not only to recruit young westerners to their cause, but also to encourage lone-wolf attacks such as those in Paris, France and San Bernardino, California. And it is their success through these unconventional soft-target attacks that has often left western leaders looking clueless.

"I don't think they're gaining strength," said President Obama in an interview with ABC Television, on November 12, 2015, one day before the Paris attacks took the world by surprise. "What is true is that from the start our goal has been first to contain, and we have contained them. They have not gained ground in Iraq. And in Syria...you don't see this systematic march by ISIL across the terrain."

But ISIS militants were not thinking about systematic marching or gaining ground in Iraq when they killed 130 persons in Paris. They simply wanted to slaughter and strike fear. Not only was it the deadliest attack on France since World War II, but even beyond those tragic consequences, it exposed the troubled relations between a decidedly dovish American Commander-in-Chief and his own top military and intelligence advisors.

"We have not contained ISIL currently," General Joseph Dunford, chairman of the Joint Chiefs of Staff, told the House Armed Services Committee two weeks after the Paris attack, directly contradicting the President after less than a month on the job.

Dunford's disagreement was nothing new. By the time he accepted the Joint Chiefs job, President Obama had time and again ignored advisors like James Mattis, Commander of the United States Central Command, Army General Lloyd Austin, top commander of U.S. forces in the Middle East, and General Martin Dempsey, Dunford's predecessor at the Joint Chiefs.

"Where the intelligence starts and stops is at the White House," said former Defense Intelligence Agency chief General Michael Flynn in an interview on Fox News Channel, referring to the agency's unheeded warnings from 2011-2012. "The president sets the priorities."[90] Nine days later, Flynn explained further to CNN's Jake Tapper. "I think that [the intelligence reports] did not meet a narrative the White House needed...I think the narrative was that al Qaeda was on the run, and (Osama) bin Laden was dead. ... They're dead and these guys are, we've beaten them," when in reality the terrorists "continue to just multiply."[91]

The President's recalcitrance about adding ground troops to his air campaign against ISIS is admired by pacifists as a principled stance, and loathed by hawks as leftist arrogance, but as these top officials' remarks make clear, it has also caused more than a little consternation within the administration's own ranks.

THE WEST'S BEST UNUSED WEAPON

The cure for such backstage confusion, and perhaps a major key to decisively defeating ISIS, may lie in exploiting a valuable asset thus far allowed to sit on the shelf. More than anyone else in the Middle East, it is the Iraqi Kurds who are the West's most loyal ally and potent weapon in the fight against ISIS. Virtually unknown outside of foreign-policy circles, they are a nation within a nation. Together with their fellow Kurds in eastern Turkey, northern Syria and northwest Iran, they comprise an invisible overlay called Greater Kurdistan. Having suffered centuries of rejection and persecution at the hands of various masters, the Kurds have developed the toughness and razor-sharp sensibilities that come from repeatedly defying the odds. But, only in Iraq they have had the chance to develop any form of self-governance, and that to stunning effect.

The history of the Kurds is long, to say the least. In fact, Erbil, the capital of Iraq's Kurdish province, boasts written records spanning 5,000 years, marking it as the world's oldest, continuously-inhabited city, having already celebrated its thousandth birthday when the biblical patriarch Abraham passed through the region some four millennia ago on his way to the "Promised Land." Additionally, Sumerian writings dating back to 3,000 B.C. reference the people of the "land of Kardo" as being fierce and cunning warriors, a description easily applied to Iraq's *Peshmerga* forces—"those who confront death"— who are respected and feared across the Middle East.

There are presently some 25-40 million ethnic Kurds spread across Turkey, Syria, Iraq and Iran, a statistic hard to pin precisely because the four countries in question are loath to admit actual numbers, lest the Kurds be emboldened. Still, if demographics defined national boundaries, the Kurd "nation" would cobble enough territory from its four hosts to render it larger than Syria, if not the consequently smaller Iraq.

If not for the much maligned Sykes-Picot agreement of World War I, today's maps might show an independent nation of Kurdistan. But in satisfying the aforementioned wish of T.E. "Lawrence of Arabia," that the postwar Middle East remain "a tissue of small jealous principalities incapable of cohesion," Britain and France denied the Kurds a promised state of their own, instead dividing them in order to ensure the fractures Lawrence desired. Such a reading of history is widely accepted, even by the Kurds themselves. The Western Allies "used us to keep the region internally unstable, so that these nations could not cause trouble for the rest of the world," a senior official from Iraq's Kurdistan Region told the authors.

It is this Kurdistan Region, with its modern history of evenhanded governance, military success, and astonishing record of peace and prosperity (while the rest of Iraq crumbled) that holds the very real potential to defeat and destroy ISIS and restore a semblance of stability to Syria, Iraq and beyond. But it is a history that might not have happened had not President George H.W. Bush been forced in 1991 to honor his rhetoric and put forth an admittedly minimal effort to protect the region.

In justifying America's recent defeat of Saddam and restoration of Kuwait's monarchy in the brief war called "Desert Storm," the 41st President, in March 1991, spoke of freedom and announced what he called a "new world order."

> Tonight in Iraq, Saddam walks amidst ruin. His war machine is crushed. His ability to threaten mass destruction is itself destroyed. His people have been lied to, denied the truth. And when his defeated legions come home, all Iraqis will see and feel the havoc he has wrought. And this I promise you: for all that Saddam has done to his own people, to the Kuwaitis, and to the entire world, Saddam and those around him are accountable...
>
> Now, we can see a new world coming into view. A world in which there is the very real prospect of a new world order. In the words of Winston Churchill, a "world order"

> in which "the principles of justice and fair play ... protect the weak against the strong ..." A world where the United Nations, freed from cold war stalemate, is poised to fulfil [sic] the historic vision of its founders. A world in which freedom and respect for human rights find a home among all nations.[92]

Bush was speaking primarily to Congress and his own nation, but as usual the whole world was listening. And as journalist Quil Lawrence points out, nowhere did the President's lofty rhetoric ring more loudly than in Iraq, where both the Kurds in the north and Shi'a in the south were emboldened to rebel against their Sunni dictator. But Saddam had not been humbled in defeat.

> Believing the American army was at their back, the Kurds and Shi'ite Arabs rose against the dictator. Fearful of empowering Iran and destabilizing the region, Bush told his half-million troops to remain behind their line in the sand. Once Saddam realized—to his amazement—that he had survived, he embarked on his last great wave of atrocities, slaughtering the rebels in the thousands.[93]

Shocked by Saddam's brazenness, and knowing that he had gassed tens of thousands of Kurds to death less than a decade earlier, Bush acted quickly to establish a no-fly zone over Kurdish territories. It was a small move, a mere gesture compared to what he could have done, but the resilient Kurds took full advantage of it. Before the world noticed, a viable Kurdistan had been born.

That the U.S. did little more than patrol the skies of northern Iraq for the next 12 years made little difference to the industrious Kurds.

Actual statehood was still a castle in the air, but at least now it was Kurdish air and they breathed it in for all they were worth.

> By early 2003, the Kurds had pushed the limits of shadow statehood as far as they could, living off blackmarket oil smuggling and whatever Saddam allowed the U.N. Oil-for-Food program to let through. Some aid organizations set up shop, but no foreign company considered investing in a country that might not be there in the morning. After half a generation in limbo, their fate wasn't clear until another accidental nation builder came along. President George W. Bush set out to finish the job his father had started, and again, unwittingly, he succeeded at a different task. The destruction of Saddam Hussein's regime and the collapse that followed left Kurdistan as the only fully functioning part of Iraq.[94]

Again, the Kurds of Iraq seized the day. While Baghdad burned and coped with snipers, in Erbil they built hotels and filled them with tourists. For every car bomb that exploded in the south, it seemed a new dealership opened in the north. And while Iraqi Prime Minister Nouri al Maliki set Shiite against Sunni and split the rest of Iraq asunder, the Kurdish government declared that henceforth their schools would no longer favor Islam, but would both tolerate and teach all religions equally.

"I would rather that a Kurd become a Christian any day than to see him become a radicalized Muslim," the region's Prime Minister, Nechirvan Barzani, told the authors in 2007. Within days, he made a similar declaration to the Washington Times, a move that may have prompted an assassination attempt against his uncle, President Massoud Barzani, weeks later. But the elder Barzani had already been just as bold.

"It is not a crime to have relations with Israel," he told the press in 2006 during an official visit to Kuwait. "Should Baghdad establish diplomatic relations with Israel, we could open a consulate in Erbil."[95]

Such tolerance of religious minorities and openness towards Israel is virtually unknown in the Muslim world, and astonishing when coming from a tribal leader like Massoud Barzani, the scion of Mustafa Barzani, the celebrated "Father of Modern Kurdistan." As the head of one of Kurdistan's two leading clans (former Iraqi President Jalal Talabani representing the other) Barzani might be expected to have bled the region's coffers and lined his own pockets, like so many other tribal leaders in his part of the world. But such an accusation would be grossly unfair to the man who, like his father before him, has pursued the safety and prosperity of Kurds everywhere.

President Barzani spends much of his time abroad, seeking support for the region's beleaguered but tireless Peshmerga troops, whom Baghdad routinely denies money and munitions sent from abroad to aid them in resisting ISIS, whose reign of terror extends to Mosul, just 50 miles west of Erbil. Meanwhile, the President's nephew, Kurdish Prime Minister Nechirvan Barzani, governs the region internally, with the assistance of the Minister of the Interior Karim Sinjari, who has served since 2001.

BOOTS ON THE GROUND

It was Interior Minister Sinjari who told the authors in early 2015 to "tell America that we will be your boots on the ground. We can defeat ISIS." That confidence was echoed hours later by Major General Aziz Waisi, commander of the elite Zerevani Peshmerga brigade.

"This is a war for all of humanity, a world war against ISIS," said Waisi in an interview with the authors. "The Peshmerga fight for humanity, not against it...And because of the Peshmerga, all of the

Sunni and Shi'a and Yazidi and other groups in Kurdistan are living in peace."

Like his superiors in Erbil, General Waisi is known to deal fairly with minorities, including the Christian refugees who fled the nearby Nineveh Plain when ISIS swept across northern Iraq and took Mosul in 2014. Waisi also directs the training of a new "Christian battalion," formed in early 2015 and comprised of about 1,000 village elders and other able-bodied Assyrian men eager to join the fight against the terrorist aggressors who drove them from their homes and land.

It was General Waisi who led the successful offensive to retake the Yazidi town of Sinjar, near the Syrian border, in November 2015. Sinjar had been held by ISIS for fifteen months, yet Waisi's Zerevani brigade took it in two days.

ISIS may have become the richest, most powerful terror organization in history, but the Peshmerga victory at Sinjar demonstrated that their fighters can be defeated quickly when western air power is combined with Peshmerga boots on the ground. And considering that Iraqi Kurdistan alone boasts 150,000 active-duty troops, there is likewise good reason to believe that cities like Mosul, Iraq and the ISIS "capital" of Raqqa, Syria can be liberated without protracted fighting.

Kurdish intelligence chief Masrour Barzani also "attributes the Sinjar triumph to Western air cover, good planning and a swiftness that surprised ISIS fighters," reported the Wall Street Journal. "'Excellent intelligence' also helped, Mr. Barzani adds, because it allowed the Kurds to defuse the jihadists' main defensive barrier, a network of remotely controlled booby traps and improvised explosive devices, before it could be detonated. Military analysts had predicted days of house-to-house combat. 'But it didn't happen,' Mr. Barzani says. It was all over in 48 hours."[96]

TO ARM OR NOT TO ARM

"To Save Iraq, Arm the Kurds," trumpeted an October 2015 New York *Times* opinion piece, answering a question already buzzing around Washington, D.C. Indeed, that view is often the one brought home by American officials and civilians alike when they return from visiting Iraq's Kurdistan Region, and in fact, more than a few have suggested helping the region achieve actual statehood. Yet, the Kurds themselves are quite aware of how precarious their situation is.

Of course, statehood has long been a dream, confided one Kurdish official off the record, before quickly adding that a federated Iraq would be far more realistic and practical. "We would prefer an Iraq with three autonomous provinces, once each for Kurds, Sunnis and Shi'a, with its capital in Baghdad," he said.

The problem with that view, of course, is that such a structure is exactly what Iraq voted to embrace in 2005, two years after the overthrow of Saddam. So hopeful was the new Iraqi Parliament that they elected a Kurd, Jalal Talabani, as their President in 2005, a year before Nouri al-Maliki, a Shi'a Muslim, became Prime Minister and set about tearing the nation apart.

Iraq then collapsed anew because the paranoid al-Maliki, in trying to rid his government of potential Sunni subversion from within, inadvertently set the stage for an ISIS invasion from without. Consequently, the terror group's numbers swelled quickly, as many of the very Sunnis whom Maliki had driven out joined Baghdadi's ranks in hopes of gaining revenge.

Thus, with ISIS far from contained, and in fact growing its numbers around the world faster than the West's air bombings can reduce them,[97] the question facing President Obama and the U.S. Congress is: Can America afford *not* to arm the Kurds?

Until very recently, the U.S. has routed nominal aid to the Kurds through official channels in Baghdad, while fully aware that the Shi'a-controlled capital—a virtual puppet of Iran—would fail to forward it to Erbil.

"If the Peshmerga want a single bullet they have to ask the Iraqi army," complained General Waisi to the authors. "In all of the Kurdistan Region, we don't have ten Humvees and no tanks. And the Kalashnikovs we have aren't very useful, but at least they will not fall into other hands...We are the ones fighting ISIS, but we need weapons given directly to us, not to Baghdad."

Persuasive though that request may seem, acceding to the General's request would produce a different set of risks.

> Baghdad and Iraqi power players worry that if Kurdistan receives direct military support from the U.S., it could push more forcefully for full independence in the future. And though some U.S. pundits and politicians have endorsed breaking up Iraq by supporting such independence, the White House has maintained throughout its nearly year-long campaign against ISIS in Iraq that it seeks to maintain the country's integrity as a state....[There are also] strategic concerns. If Iraq were to split into three segments...the Islamic State could further consolidate its power and its hold on Iraqi Sunni Arabs by stoking tensions between the bitter neighbors....{Likewise} earlier this year, Shiite leaders threatened renewed sectarian violence when they heard about a congressional proposal to recognize Iraq's Kurds and Sunnis as "countries" so Washington could directly arm them.[98]

But is there any longer an Iraq to maintain? "The Islamic State has made the 'One Iraq' policy obsolete," argue Aliza Marcus and Andrew Apostolou, authors of the New York *Times* article.

> If American policy wants to be truly effective, it should do more than just give a few weapons and limited training. Instead, the United States must help Kurdistan to organize, train and equip a nonpolitical Kurdish army....Given what the Kurds have already achieved with so little, a properly trained and equipped Kurdish army would likely inflict significant damage on the Islamic State. This would prevent the Islamic State from entrenching its control over northwestern Iraq and relieve pressure on the Iraqi government. Crucially, that should provide Prime Minister Haider al-Abadi of Iraq with the breathing space he needs to reform and properly rebuild his own forces.
>
> With Russian military intervention in the Middle East growing, President Obama needs to strengthen his Kurdish ally, which has demonstrated an authentic commitment to the anti-Islamic State campaign in Iraq. A Kurdish army able to fight the Islamic State more seriously is the only way to achieve victory without sending American soldiers back to the battlefield.[99]

No one can hope to completely destroy the virulent strain of Salafism—*aka* Wahhabism—that is growing so rapidly within Sunni Islam. But the destruction of ISIS would go a long way to stopping its violent momentum, and in this case, necessity is the mother of intervention. Someone has to fight ISIS, and thus far the Kurds seem more willing and able than anyone else to do so. Moreover, after a dozen years of working closely with Iraq's Kurdish authorities in distributing humanitarian aid—often under the close watch of the Peshmerga—the authors believe they are more than up to the task. Additionally, with some allies unwilling to step up, while others like Turkey and Saudi Arabia play both sides of the table, the case for arming Iraq's Kurds is made even stronger.

It would be foolish for America to put all her military eggs in one basket, and the Kurdish option carries no guarantees, but it is certainly a better one than most others when it comes to defeating ISIS on their home territory.

TURKISH BETRAYAL AND KURDISH LOYALTY

One reason the Kurds of Iraq are so eager to be America's boots on the ground is that their conflict with ISIS, while a battle for their survival, also presents them with the opportunity to finally establish their place in the world as a people. The deservedly maligned Sykes-Picot Agreement of World War I that chopped Kurdistan into pieces and parceled it out to Turkey, Syria, Iraq and Iran, was nothing new. Throughout their 5,000-year history, the Kurds have been dismissed as the ethnic left-overs of everyone else in the region.

"We are always part of other nations and our contributions are always attributed to other nations," a Kurdish professor lamented in an interview with Steven Mansfield, author of *The Miracle of the Kurds*. "We are indistinguishable from other nations. Some of the great figures of history—Cyrus the Great or Cyaxares or Darius or Saladin—all are Kurds but all are remembered as belonging to other peoples."[100]

Over the years since the end of the Great War, the U.S. has continued the practice of France and Britain, shunning the Kurds in favor of Turkey, its NATO ally since 1952, despite that nation's systematic discrimination—and sometimes outright persecution—of its Kurdish population. This has resulted in a sense of abandonment amongst the Kurds of Turkey, and after a century of uncontested repression, they are a more cynical and hostile people than their kinsmen in Iran, Syria and, especially, Iraq. As a result, a westerner attempting to learn about "the Kurds" might read in one place about Kurdish terrorists known as the PKK, and in another place see them called America's allies.

The United States' apathy towards the plight of Kurds in general makes the indefatigable loyalty of Iraq's Kurds all the more remarkable. And that loyalty, combined with their record of stability and overall prosperity during the rest of Iraq's collapse, is a good predictor of their reliability should the U.S. arm them to fight ISIS.

SO, WHAT ARE *YOUR* OPTIONS?

Just as the Kurds are ready and able to defend their homeland, the age of entrepreneurial warfare demands that ordinary Americans prepare to defend their homes and towns as well. But how? How can you protect yourself and your family right there where you live? Is your town the next San Bernardino?

There are answers to those questions—perhaps not perfect or foolproof and certainly not complete—but they are good, solid answers nonetheless. In a moment, you can turn the page and read them for yourself, or maybe even add to or improve them. But even before you read on, know this one thing:

There is hope.

10

NINE STEPS AMERICA'S LEADERS CAN TAKE NOW

"A good plan violently executed now is better than a perfect plan executed next week."

GENERAL GEORGE PATTON

War changes everything, but it especially changes minds. During World War II, Americans rallied to the cause and lived sacrificially in order to help defeat the nation's enemies. Even then, the homeland itself remained safe from attack. Rosie the riveter could walk or take a bus to work without keeping an ear out for sirens or the whistling of falling bombs. Children could play stickball in city streets or roam the country woods without fear of straying too far from a bomb shelter Dad had dug and stocked behind the house.

Life in London from 1939-1945 was quite another story. More than a million of the city's homes were destroyed by German bombs. Food and clothing were rationed via coupons. Cabbage patches replaced flower gardens, and nearly every vacant lot became a vegetable cooperative. Children played less outdoors to preserve wear and tear on their clothing, and when they did leave the house, it was either with hoe in hand or to head for the bomb shelter out back, where the family often slept anyway. Londoners lacking their own shelters got used to sleeping in subway ticket halls, platforms and even in the train tunnels themselves. Everyone, including babies, wore identity tags or metal bracelets to make it easier to identify bodies if the worst happened. It was, perhaps, the specter of death in those tags that—more than anything else—caused tens of thousands of parents to evacuate their children to relatives, friends or even willing strangers in the British countryside.[101]

War changes everything.

As this book goes to press, ISIS is making its deadly presence known in America. No, Chicago has not been reduced to rubble and sirens do not sound in New York City. But the frequency of lone-wolf attacks in places like Boston, Massachusetts and San Bernardino, California, as well as increased warnings about "sleeper cells," have set the nation's teeth on edge. Americans still sleep in their bedrooms, but restively. Gun sales skyrocket. Skittish school superintendents keep careful watch, and sometimes a single threatening email has shut down schools and cost a city millions of dollars.

So what can—what *must*—America do to defeat ISIS? More importantly, what can you do, right now, as soon as you finish this book?

This chapter and the next contain two lists of action steps culled from what the authors believe is the wisest advice from dozens of scholars and hundreds of editorials and opinion columns, published on every available medium. These lists are not perfect, of course, but to echo General George Patton, a good plan vigorously executed now is better than a perfect plan executed next week.

NINE STEPS AMERICA'S LEADERS CAN TAKE NOW

1. *Admit that America is at war with radical Islamist jihadists.*

President George W. Bush declared a "war on terror," but aside from countering propaganda with propaganda, it is impossible to wage war against a concept. Concepts do not behead people. They do not blow themselves up in order to kill bystanders. Terrorists do those things. In this instance, a specific group of terrorists that calls itself the Islamic State is making war on America and other western nations in the name of Islam. It is certainly not the brand of Islam that is practiced by peace-loving Muslim Americans, but it is nonetheless warfare conducted under the banner of Islamic jihad—holy war. And the first thing U.S. leaders need to do—regardless of political affiliations—is to admit that ISIS is a theologically and politically motivated foe with whom America is at war. No more euphemisms like workplace violence. This is war.

2. ***Destroy ISIS militarily in Iraq and Syria, and take away their caliphate.***

ISIS' alleged caliphate physically consists of a portion of Syria and Iraq roughly the size of the state of Indiana, but its sheer existence holds a hypnotic appeal for radical Muslims around the world, and undoubtedly motivates many of them either to join the fight there or to wage jihad independently wherever they are.

There are supposedly two sides to every argument, but in the case of mobilizing troops to dismantle the caliphate there are three. Some pundits advocate isolating ISIS and cutting off the caliphate's supply lines until it rots from within. The counter-argument is that jihadism knows no borders. ISIS now exists in the form of independent franchises in at least 20 nations, and although strangling their supply lines in Raqqa, Syria and Mosul, Iraq is necessary, it would do nothing to stop new chapters from popping up like gophers somewhere else. The terror group's early-2016 build-up to 6,500 fighters in Libya is a case in point.

Others take the position that American "interventionism" has caused more problems than it has solved and that the U.S. should pull out of the Middle East permanently. The most common rebuttal of this argument: "If we don't fight them over there, we'll have to fight them here."

The authors support the increasingly common third option: Prosecute a ground war that augments a more locally commanded air campaign. As previously stated, we believe the Iraqi Kurds could then field sufficient forces to eradicate ISIS in Iraq. Whether or not they are willing to cross the border and fight in Syria is another matter. Certainly that notion risks raising the ire of Turkish authorities who do not want to embolden the 19 million Kurds who inhabit their eastern region, and who may try and saw off territory for a state of their own. But driving ISIS out of Iraq would liberate millions of people and shrink both the terrorists' domain and egos.

Most analysts who advocate waging a ground war also insist that it be prosecuted by a multinational coalition comprised of the strongest western nations, along with those regional allies to whom ISIS poses an existential threat. The recently announced 34-nation Arab coalition—assuming it is more than a charade—makes such a plan more viable. Several experts also strongly advocate removing Syrian dictator Bashar al-Assad and paving the way for his replacement, although that idea immediately evokes memories of what happened when dictators Muammar Gaddafi and Saddam Hussein were deposed in Libya and Iraq, only to see those nations fall into even worse chaos after the fact.

Despite the possible pitfalls, three steps can be taken at once:

» Lift environmental restrictions that currently prevent the bombing of oil fields and other resources from which ISIS derives massive financial benefit.

» Replace Washington's bureaucratic "kill chain" with forward-deployed air controllers in Syria to call in airstrikes. Superior intelligence will better pinpoint enemy locations, reduce civilian casualties and dramatically speed up decision making by the pilots themselves.

» By any means necessary, stop both Syria and Turkey from buying a single drop of oil from ISIS on the black market. In Syria, such a move would hurt both Assad and ISIS, and incentivize the population to rise up against both of their oppressors.

3. *Secure America's borders.*

America's 1,933-mile southern border is also her most porous, and the time for debate about how open or closed it should be has passed. Government watchdog Judicial Watch claims to possess intelligence proving that ISIS has at least one training camp in Mexico within eight miles of the U.S. border. That claim is backed up by several members of Congress, most notably Tennessee Representative Marsha Blackburn, but strongly denied by the Department of Homeland Security. One fact beyond dispute, however, renders the discussion moot: ISIS has declared its intent to infiltrate the United States by every available means, at every possible entry point. In light of that fact, several steps can be taken:

» Deploy every available human, electronic and material resource in guarding the southern border, while also issuing appropriate warnings—the kind with consequences—to Mexico.

» Reform America's fraud-ridden visa policies. According to the Department of Homeland Security, nearly 500,000 foreign visitors overstayed their visas in the United States in 2015 alone.[102] Moreover, that figure only accounts for four of the nearly 200 types of visas available to immigrants and visitors to the United States, including three categories that are particularly vulnerable to exploitation by terrorists: visas for temporary workers (H1-B), visas for foreign fiancées of American citizens (K1) and student visas (F, J and M). When the 2015 H1-B visa application window opened on April 1 of that year, Congress' entire quota of 65,000 visas was filled within days. And as is typical of Washington when facing a glut, it was not the government that vetted and processed the permits, but corporate managers and lawyers so eager to put them to work that the vast majority were not vetted at all. Similar abuse of the K1 fiancée visa legally admitted terrorist Tashfeen Malik to the USA in the months before she and husband Syed Rizwan Farook killed 14 and injured 22 in San Bernardino, California. As to the number of students abusing the system, the latest obtainable numbers show that nearly 60,000 remained in the U.S. after their visas expired in 2014.[103] With only 7,000 Immigration and Customs Enforcement agents to monitor well over a half million visa violators, ISIS' Caliph Ibrahim must sleep with a smile. But Washington should not, and although both the President and Congress are taking steps to make these visas more difficult and expensive to obtain,[104] the sad testimony of San Bernardino shows that their rewritten immigration laws of both 2013 and 2015 were far from effective.

» Implement enhanced security screening in the U.S. Immigration and Customs Enforcement agency (ICE). Add an extra layer of interviews for anyone visiting or emigrating from a Muslim nation. This is especially important in light of the fact that from 2012 through the end of 2015, more than 102,000 refugees have entered the U.S. from Syria alone.[105] That number almost certainly includes ISIS sympathizers or infiltrators, as evidenced in Germany by hundreds of rapes and other attacks committed by refugees during that country's 2016 New Year's celebrations.

- Engage in thorough behavioral profiling via every medium, including social media pages that in the past were astonishingly ignored by explicit order of the Director of Homeland Security. America's Constitutional rights, including an implied right to privacy, do not extend to non-citizens, especially with regard to social-media posts that are published to the general public.
- Ban the Muslim brotherhood and similar radical groups within the physical boundaries of the United States, and revoke the citizenship of any American known to preach jihad, or who is in direct contact with ISIS, Hamas, Hezbollah or other proven terror groups.

4. ***Bolster friendly Middle East alliances and punish hypocrites.***

Jordan and Israel have proven themselves to be reliable allies in the Middle East, as have Egypt and Turkey, though to a lesser extent. Such nations should be heralded and supported, although Turkey must confine its attacks to ISIS, not Turkish Kurds.[106] In Egypt, President Abdel Fattah el-Sisi has spoken boldly against Islamist extremism since overthrowing his predecessor in a 2013 coup, yet that extremism persists in his own country, especially amongst disillusioned and impressionable young males who easily fall prey to ISIS propaganda. Others supposed allies such as Saudi Arabia, Qatar and Kuwait have played both sides of the ISIS equation, because they see less risk in quietly defying the U.S. than in cracking down on extremism within their own borders.

So, what can be done about this particular state of affairs?

- Call on Muslim states to renounce all forms of Shari'ah expansionism.

- Withdraw all funding from those states that refuse to cooperate, or who fail to stanch the flow of funds from their financial systems to ISIS.
- Insist that neighboring nations offer safe haven to refugees currently immigrating to the West.
- Stand firmly and openly with persecuted minorities such as Christians and Yazidis and tie all commerce and financial aid directly to their treatment.
- Extend humanitarian aid to victims of ISIS, but in a measured way that does not promote dependency. As much as possible, the U.S. should rely on non-governmental organizations to oversee such efforts (see Epilogue).
- Encourage support of non-governmental organizations that are committed for the long term to build schools and hospitals in lands ravaged by ISIS.

5. ***Break with Iran and advocate for a truly independent Federated Iraq.***

The Grand Ayatollah of Iran and his government drool over the prospect of an ISIS-free Iraq. Additionally, Iran remains a leading sponsor of terror attacks around the world, rivaled only by ISIS. This rogue state's confidence is bolstered in no small part by the impunity with which they act. For example, the U.S. State Department has admitted that Iran did not even sign the Joint Comprehensive Plan of Action (*aka* The Iran Nuclear Agreement) in July 2015.[107] It is thus a unilateral American commitment, not an agreement. This is why the Iranian regime has consistently defied its terms, pursuing offensive nuclear capabilities at full speed and with impunity, persisting in its claim that the nation of Israel has no right to exist, and actively sponsoring the anti-Israel terror groups Hamas and Hezbollah.

Additionally, as the most dominant Shi'a Muslim nation in the world, Iran has, since 2006, gradually subjugated southern Iraq to such an extent that some Iranian officials have referred to Baghdad as the capital of the "Empire of Iran."[108]

What steps can the United States take to prevent Iran from profiting from the demise of ISIS?

» Abandon the so-called joint nuclear agreement at once, and actively encourage regime change in Iran.

» Consider military action such as surgical strikes that will cripple Iran's nuclear ambitions.

» Push hard against Iranian influence in the Iraqi government, and reject cooperation with Iranian military efforts in Iraq.

» Strongly advocate for a true, federated Iraq consisting of three autonomous provinces: a Shi'a province in the south, a Sunni province in the west and a Kurdish province in the north, each with equal voices in the capital of Baghdad.

» Pressure Baghdad to fully welcome both the Sunnis of Anbar and Iraq's Kurds to participate in a vigorous joint military effort against ISIS, with the threat to otherwise encourage independence for the Kurdistan Region.

6. *Wage all-out cyber-warfare against ISIS.*

ISIS has thus far outmaneuvered the USA in cyberspace because it has exploited the Internet entrepreneurially versus America's bloated bureaucracy. Adding injury to insult, while the U.S. Department of Homeland Security was prohibiting American intelligence from examining individual Facebook pages, ISIS was discovered in late 2015 to have invented its own smartphone app, complete with encryption capabilities.[109] Once again, in Washington, D.C., political correctness had won the day but lost the battle. The Internet has been one of ISIS' most potent weapons, and the U.S. must act quickly and definitively against them in at least four ways:

- Invade ISIS' Internet safe havens and disrupt their communications.
- Recruit hackers like the group known as Anonymous, who declared its own "full-scale cyber war" against ISIS in mid-2015, taking down some 2,000 of the terror group's Twitter accounts almost immediately.[110]
- Pressure Twitter, Apple and other communications software providers to police and aggressively enforce their terms of service, and to widely publicize their success in catching violators.
- Put the issue of intelligence gathering versus privacy rights to a referendum on the November 2016 election ballot.

7. ***Wage a massive counter-propaganda campaign against ISIS.***

As noted in Chapter 5, ISIS has been alarmingly successful in recruiting foreign fighters, preying in particular upon disillusioned youth in the West. Therefore, in addition to waging war against ISIS' Internet capabilities, the U.S. should counter the group's propaganda, utilizing its own psychological weaponry against it. As a start, here are six suggestions from a variety of experts:

- Utilize all social media platforms from texting to live-streamed broadcasts.
- Adopt meaningful language, slogans, icons and imagery that ISIS' main recruitment pool finds attractive.

- Expose ISIS as thugs, murderers and monsters, exploiting every possible human-interest angle.
- Portray ISIS as parasites, capable only of destroying but not building. Magnify and mock their failures, discrediting even their smallest lies.
- Publicize the various passages of the Qur'an that contradict ISIS' philosophy and deeds.
- Amplify the voices of former jihadists and other ISIS opposition. Enlist defectors to speak against them.

8. ***Encourage Muslim Reformers.***

Muslims and non-Muslims the world over must face one crucial fact: only Muslims can reform Islam. Yet, for a time after the rise of ISIS, it seemed that these reformers were afraid to speak up, purposely ignored or simply lost in the noise. Thankfully, that is no longer the case. Today, the voices of Islamic reform are speaking out both eloquently and with courage, among the more prominent of them:

- Attorney Khurram Dara, author of *Contracting Fear: Islamic Law in the Middle East and Middle America.*[111]
- Emory University Law Professor Abdullahi Ahmed An-Na'im, an expert in international law, comparative law, human rights and Islamic law.[112]
- Women's rights advocate Professor Ayaan Hirsi Ali, whose 2015 work, *Heretic: Why Islam Needs a Reformation Now*[113] is among the clearest and most specific works thus far available.
- King Abdullah of Jordan and Egyptian President Abdel Fattah el-Sisi, both of whom have boldly and passionately called for reform in the Islamic world.

Such bravery should be given every available platform from Senate hearings to national television, and afforded protection as needed.

9. ***Educate and assist Muslim communities in combatting ISIS' recruiting efforts.***

Muslim Americans often fail to speak against ISIS not because they are closet sympathizers but because they are afraid of reprisals. Added to their fear is the fact—spotlighting this is the height of political incorrectness—that many do not know what the Qur'an actually says any better than Roman Catholics and evangelical Christians know what the Bible says. The truth is, labels like Muslim, Catholic and Baptist most often describe people's religious heritage, not their ability to explain their faith. This theological deficit is particularly dangerous to the Islamic community everywhere, because ISIS presents prospective recruits with a thorough philosophical explanation for their cause. It is a selective philosophy riddled with lies and inconsistencies, but lacking refutation, the ISIS apologetic offers meaning and purpose to young people in search of both.

Besides fear and ignorance, there is another danger that, while common to all American families, is especially perilous for Muslim Americans: *an unsupervised Internet.* As cited previously, ISIS recruiters surf social media platforms in search of Internet-savvy young people whose parents, far less knowledgeable than they, are incapable of monitoring their children's contacts. As a result, many sons and daughters have been radicalized right under their parents' noses. No case is more instructive than that of alleged San Bernardino terror accomplice Enrique Marquez, a 24-year old man who lived with his mother. "He's a good person," she assured reporters, yet claimed to be unaware of her son's 2011 conversion to Islam, as well as his more recent marriage to a

Russian woman (possibly a paid arrangement in exchange for helping the woman pursue residency in the U.S.).

Regardless of age-of-consent laws, every homeowner or head of household in America is responsible to secure computer networks and their usage within the walls of their own homes. This is doubly important in families that, in demographic terms, are prime targets of ISIS recruiters. With the awareness that "terrorists only have to succeed one time," such vulnerability is a matter of national security. But that does not mean that it should be left to the federal government to accomplish. Instead, there are steps that America's leaders should encourage Muslim families to take.

» Guide concerned parents and individuals to local, private organizations that help troubled youth.

» Guide Muslim families towards the writings and videos of respected Muslim reformers.

» Encourage the Muslim community to uniformly reject silence and actively inform local authorities at the first hint of trouble.

» Monitor their children's media usage, friendships and free time.

This chapter has suggested nine action steps America's leaders can take right now, but regardless of government action or inertia, there are also several sensible steps that you can take starting now. Whatever action you take, remember that your voice should ring loudest in the halls of Congress and the White House. Whether you agree or disagree with the authors' conclusions, you must speak up. You must act.

11

NINE STEPS YOU CAN TAKE NOW

"Silence in the face of evil is itself evil. God will not hold us guiltless. Not to speak is to speak. Not to act is to act."

DIETRICH BONHOEFFER

Truth is always a friend, but it is not always friendly. At the moment, the unfriendly truth is that ISIS is already active in America, and tuning in to a good football game or going about business as usual will not make it go away. Nor can we simply say, "the government needs to take care of this." These terrorists have declared war on *you and your family*, and you must take action not only to defend your loved ones, but also to help defeat the enemy in America's own back yard. Moreover, ISIS might be the world's most dangerous terror group *thus far*, but it will not be the last. The world has changed and you must adjust to a new reality. There are no shortcuts.

First, some reckoning: Do you know who your children's (or roommate's) online "friends" really are? Does the idea of owning guns or gas masks strike you as sensible or absurd? If a San Bernardino or Paris-style attack happened in your town today, would your opinion about guns change?

With the exception of September 2001, American civilians have not had to rally to defend their homeland since World War II, and prepping for action seventy-five years later will require a significant mental and spiritual adjustment, not only inside Washington's Beltway but from border to border. For one thing, the world has come a long way from the days of a kamikaze attack that could strike only one target within a limited distance. Nobody has to fly a noisy *Yokosuka* dive-bomber hundreds of miles beneath the radar to reach your house. You live in the age of entrepreneurial warfare, of exploding vests, suitcase bombs and ricin powder. And with such frightfully unguarded borders—both physical and spiritual— the authors would be less than honest if we did not encourage you to pray for divine mercy, grace and wisdom, not only for yourself but also for the nation (see Epilogue.)

There are also several concrete steps that both praying and non-praying Americans can take. There is nothing magical about them, but several have been so delegitimized by the bullies of political correctness—the other face of bigotry—that they are often overlooked.

NINE STEPS YOU CAN TAKE RIGHT NOW

1. ***Educate yourself.***

ISIS owes its "success" in large part to the fact that the West has repeatedly underestimated the depths of its motivation and determination. From Washington's blind insistence that the group "has nothing to do with Islam" to Europe's passivity to Islamist immigrants' refusal to assimilate, a 2006 speech by the late Libyan dictator Muammar Gaddafi is proving all too prophetic: "There are signs that Allah will grant Islam victory in Europe—without swords, without guns, without conquests. The 50 million Muslims of Europe will turn it into a Muslim continent within a few decades."[114]

Equally dangerous is bigoted oversimplification of the threat. Declarations that "all Muslims are dangerous" on the one hand and dismissing ISIS' capabilities and reach on the other both amount to psychological comfort foods that momentarily quash the hunger for answers but do nothing to get you into shape.

There is no substitute for educating yourself, and the authors commend you for your decision to read this book. But remember, *Unmasking ISIS* is only a guide, not an encyclopedia. In order to further inform yourself, we recommend the following initial steps, used in tandem with the resources cited in the Endnotes of this book.

- » Use the Qur'an and the Bible to objectively compare the words of Muhammad and Jesus, both of whom Islam considers prophets. Afterward, ask yourself: Would Jesus have followed or approved of Muhammad, as Muslims universally insist? Are the two religions they founded morally equivalent? There are articles and books promoting both Yes and No answers to these questions. Don't rely on flashy websites. Compare the opposing views of the more scholarly authors like Karen Armstrong on the one hand and Robert Spencer on the other (see Bibliography).

- » Whether you are Muslim or non-Muslim, read the passages in the Qur'an and Hadith that ISIS leader Abu Bakr al-Baghdadi uses to justify violent jihad—and determine whether or not *you* agree that ISIS "has nothing to do with Islam." Or is author Ayaan Hirsi Ali correct that violent jihad is "an ideology imbedded in Islam itself"?[115] Don't accept sound bite answers. Settling the issue in your own mind will help you take more meaningful action.

- » Inform yourself regularly using varied sources, from MSNBC to Fox News Network on television and from *Huffington Post* to Glenn Beck's *The Blaze* online. You may prefer one side over the other, but make sure to listen thoughtfully to parties with whom you disagree.

» Monitor online foreign news and information sources from Europe and the Middle East, most of whom maintain English-language websites. Such sources not only broaden your information base, but also allow you to see how the rest of the world views America's efforts in fighting ISIS. Make sure to include freelance war journalists like Michael Yon[116] and photographer Nicole Tung.[117]

2. *Insist that news media report the news honestly.*

» The First Amendment in the Constitution's Bill of Rights guarantees, amongst other forms of expression, freedom of the press. Why? "When our forefathers established special guarantees for the freedom of the press," wrote President Harry Truman in 1952, "they did so not for the personal aggrandizement of the publishers, but to serve the public."[118]

» The press has been called America's "fourth estate" because collectively it wields nearly as much power as a fourth branch of civil government. Even in this age of instant information and millions of blogs published over a decentralized Internet, a handful of news agencies and interconnected networks still dominate the reporting of news. Yet, today most news media lean so transparently to the cultural right or left that the public is left scratching its head, wondering if anyone is telling the truth. Meanwhile, ISIS does not care about sides, except to exploit the weaknesses of both. Thus, it is more important than ever that—pundits notwithstanding—editors and journalists alike report the facts about ISIS without political spin.

» What is the remedy for biased media? News organizations care about ratings the way politicians care about votes, and when enough people write letters or make telephone calls, they tremble. Don't wait for pollsters to call you. "Vote early; vote often" isn't allowed in politics, but it's pure magic with news media. Among other things, your calls and emails can pressure local and national newsrooms to jettison political correctness and stick to hard facts about ISIS. Ask them to broadcast interviews with Muslim reformers and stories that feature Muslims and non-Muslims such as Christians and Jews who are working cooperatively for the cause of peace.[119]

3. *Take pride in America's heritage, traditions and values.*

In the immediate aftermath of the September 2001 attacks, multitudes of Americans—especially New Yorkers—displayed awe-inspiring courage and compassion. Yet, within days, a chorus of professional naysayers began pushing the pendulum with all its might to the opposite extreme, to try and make America herself the villain of 9/11. The bombings had been a "monstrous dose of reality" for a nation more "cowardly" than its al Qaeda attackers, opined Susan Sontag in *The New Yorker* on September 24.[120] Predictable "blowback" against American imperialism, said author Chalmers Johnson three days later in *The Nation*.[121] It took a full three years for antiwar filmmaker Michael Moore to set his screed to film with *Fahrenheit 9/11*, and from there the flogging of America has continued, pausing only when an attack in Boston, Paris or San Bernardino renders it temporarily unprofitable.

Thankfully, post-2001 Internet innovations such as YouTube, Facebook, Twitter and self-publishing have broken the media monopoly, and today a counter-chorus of ordinary citizens is raising its collective voice to declare, "We're tired of being shamed by snobs and are thankful to be Americans." You can join that chorus.

» Express yourself in speech that is grounded in gratitude for your freedom to do so.

- When you find yourself in the company of soldiers and veterans, honor them in tangible ways, even if you disagree with America's war efforts.
- Find history books older than yourself and reread the story of the United States from a more traditional perspective. They are not necessarily bias free but generally they are less tainted by cynicism.
- Read the Founders in their own words. No, they were not all saints in powdered wigs, but their collective wisdom in establishing the republic and attempting to ensure its future was profound.
- If you're a parent, teach your children what you know about America's history, from the brilliance of the U.S. Constitution to the shame of slavery. Don't leave that duty to strangers and school boards.
- Monitor your local public schools and hold them accountable for what children where you live are taught in history, social studies and other subjects.

4. ***Don't only care about the victims of ISIS. Care for them.***

"I have seen that you Americans are a good people," the Syriac Archbishop of Mosul told the authors in April 2015. Now living as a refugee in Erbil, Kurdistan, he was preparing to lead the 10,000 members of his diocese in an outdoor Easter liturgy that, for the first time in 2,000 years, would not take place in Mosul.

"You Americans show compassion," he said, "even rescuing lost dogs and cats. But we are the world's oldest Christian community, still speaking Aramaic, the language of Jesus. Yet we are forgotten. Please," he continued, his voice breaking. "My people have lost everything. We would be happy if you only treat us like lost cats."

The authors promised to relay his Eminence's pleas, and we

encourage you to support relief organizations that are honest and efficient in getting food, clothing and other needed supplies all the way to the people in need.

5. *Support non-governmental organizations (NGOs) whose aid is geared for the longer term.*

The aphorism that "good governments don't make good men; good men make good governments" is especially true with regard to war-torn nations that need rebuilding. NGOs have proven far more efficient than government bureaucracies in helping to reconstruct vital institutions such as hospitals, schools and businesses, and even in advising incoming governments themselves.

Beyond helping with emergency relief efforts, you should consider supporting NGOs dedicated to providing long term structural help. In post-ISIS times they will be indispensable to securing the future peace of Syria, Iraq and other Middle East nations. Armies may win the peace, but only compassion with its sleeves rolled up can win a culture.

6. *Befriend "the other."*

Although it is perfectly natural for people to associate with others like themselves—that is how communities usually form in the first place—you now live in a nation whose fabric is tearing. Government mandates and programs will inevitably attempt to fill the vacuum when private efforts are lacking, but they are by nature inefficient, top-down undertakings that ultimately cannot heal a nation any more than nails can heal a wound.

The current crisis calls for Americans to befriend Americans *unlike* themselves, and to listen more than speak. Forget winning arguments. Forget holding community forums and town halls to air your opinions. Instead, get to know the Muslim next door, the young black man who eats at the same fast-food place you frequent, or the white guy with a rifle in the rear window of his truck. Get to know someone you normally would avoid. Share your table, not to convince yourself how open-minded you are but simply to make a friend. Then, gradually, let the bond of relationship become a bridge for discussion, but only after being friends has become more important to both of you than being right.

7. ***Hold your representatives at all levels of government to account.***

Regardless of how much bureaucracies, regulations and tax rates may have interfered with your life, the U.S. Constitution says your government works for you. You, along with the "you" next door and the "you" across town, collectively are the employer to whom mayors, governors, lawmakers and even Presidents must give account. So do your job.

Google what your Congressman and Senators propose to do about ISIS, and then write polite, to-the-point emails and make phone calls to express your opinion. Do the same with your mayor and local council members, and with the local and state police. Then write more emails and place more phone calls.

Above all else, vote. Take time to find out who and what issues are on the ballot and don't let anything keep you away from the polls on election day.

The point is this: You may not be interested in politics but politics is interested in you. Ultimately, the collective You can strongly influence what Washington must do to defeat ISIS, and what your local authorities have to do to protect your town. But you will have to speak loudly enough to be heard above the Beltway machine.

You *are* America. The homeland is your front line. Do your job.

8. ***Learn how to defend your home and family.***

What can you do to protect your loves ones in the age of ISIS? Your first line of defense is not a gun in your bedroom. It is the computer in the living room, the laptop in your teenaged daughter's bedroom or perhaps even the smartphone in the jeans pocket of your adult son still living under your roof.[122] Each of these devices, if unsupervised, is a national border as porous as the one between Texas and Mexico, especially considering that children's and teens' electronic "screen time" now averages 50 hours per week.[123] That's the equivalent of a full work week spent in an often unsupervised cyber world that, for millions of parents, might as well be New York City, Disney World or—as has happened too many times—Raqqa, Syria, where the "cute guy" who just friended your loved one on social media is actually chumming for the caliphate.

Here are practical steps you can take to protect your home and family in the Age of ISIS:

» Learn the ins and outs of Internet security for yourself, and personally choose your home network's master password, one that is secure but not impossible for *you* to remember. Don't trust the tech geek who's going to forget it the moment he climbs back into his van.

» Invest in software and hardware that can shield every online device in your home from intrusion. Beyond computers, this includes Wi-Fi thermostats and baby monitors, both of which could render your home vulnerable in case of a massive online terror attack.

» Educate your family members and loved ones about the "new reality" of life in America. No one wants to frighten their own children, but neither should you leave them ignorant and vulnerable. Teach everyone in your family what to watch for when they're online or out and about town. This is discretion, not paranoia. Set the rules for online use in your home, regardless of how young or old the other residents may be. Lovingly explain that it's your house, your responsibility—your rules.

» Don't let anyone else's opinion govern your conscience. Purchase the protective gear you think you need, as well as home security equipment you can monitor and control. Ensure that everyone at home is trained to use whatever you choose safely and wisely. Don't feel foolish in doing these things. In an era of portable mass destruction, even gas masks aren't just for camouflaged crazies anymore.

9. *All Americans, including Muslims, should stay watchful and speak up. Don't let a simplistic fear of profiling or retribution silence you.*

Medical authorities say that a high percentage of fatal heart attacks could be prevented by taking swift action instead of wishing symptoms away as "probably indigestion" or insisting that "I'll be okay."

The same principle holds for acting on suspected terrorist activity, as was evident in December 2015, when a neighbor of San Bernardino terrorist Syed Farook failed to report weeks of suspicious movements in and out of Farook's home, because he did not want to racially profile him.[124] The neighbor's reluctance is understandable; no one can justify such profiling. But ignoring suspicious activity on ethnic grounds is as dangerous as suspecting it on those same grounds. Ethnicity, like language, is occasionally a common characteristic of violent groups but *it is never a cause.* Indeed, the same ground rules for reporting suspicious activity should apply to white Americans as to people of color or obvious middle-eastern or Asian origin.

Unlike ethnicity, religion involves choice, and therefore it sometimes—but not always—is a motivating force for violence. Even here, however, *the cause of violence is always choice,* even if that choice is based on religion. Thus, the false equivalence of saying that because all ISIS terrorists are Sunni Muslims, therefore all Sunni Muslims are ISIS terrorists is no more legitimate than equating Winston Churchill with

Adolph Hitler because both were white men who professed Christianity and led their nations in fighting World War II.

The problem of profiling involves knowing when and under what circumstances you should speak up. And the answer lies in being aware of people's actions, neither favoring nor discounting their ethnicity, nationality or religion, and then notifying the appropriate authorities when you believe it it is warranted.

THE IMPORTANCE OF *ISM*

Just as there is a stark difference between community and communism, or triumph and triumphalism, there is also a wide gap between Islam and Islamism. *Ism* is what turns a concept into a cause. Some causes are admirable, but quite often an *ism* can become a cancer that transforms the good into something grotesque.

In America, secularism has made war on religion in the name of neutrality and rendered the public square functionally atheist in many cities and most schools.

It is Islamism that ISIS embraces...in the name of Islam. Islamism blows up children in the name of righteousness, turns cities into prisons, homes into torture chambers, Kurds into lab rats for chemical weapons testing, marriage into rape and heaven into an orgy.

Unmasking ISIS has been about exposing Islamism and exploring ways to defeat the monster that is ISIS. It is not an effort to reform Islam itself—only Islam's ummah can do that—nor about destroying the ideology that spawns an al Qaeda, a Boko Haram or an ISIS. Hydra will show another face, and another, until it too is put to death. Yes, even Hydra can die.

In the Greek myth, Hercules killed the Hydra only after his faithful charioteer, Iolaus, stepped-in to seal by fire each wound before it could grow two new heads. But you've probably never heard of Iolaus, have you? Hercules is the only hero people remember, the one for whom books are written and movies made. But Iolaus was a hero, too, with smaller muscles and less publicity, but with fire in his hand.

The world, more than likely, has never heard of you either. But you can still be the hero, even if they don't remember. All that remains is to find the fire inside you, not the fire of hate but the fire of courage that destroys hate.

Find your fire. Get out of your chariot. Be the hero.

EPILOGUE

A CALL TO CHASE THE STORM

"As the people stood in the distance, Moses approached the dark cloud where God was."

EXODUS 20:21

As Syria's civil war passes its five year mark, the nation's death toll stands at some 470,000, nearly twice the number estimated only eighteen months earlier. In neighboring Iraq, nearly 20,000 civilians have lost their lives in less than two years of fighting ISIS, and millions have been displaced, especially to the north, in Mosul and the nearby Nineveh Plain. Once home to hundreds of thousands of Christians, the plundered towns and villages of the plain lie forsaken, their residents having taken refuge in cities like Dohuk and Erbil, the Kurdish capital, whose infrastructure sags under the weight of caring for them. But care they do, and indeed, the friendship between Iraq's Kurds and Christians is one bright spot in an overall sea of darkness.

In 2015, while we were conducting research in Erbil, a young Peshmerga soldier named Abdullah asked to speak with us. A week earlier, he had been on the front lines fighting ISIS and was now on leave for a few nights at his sister's home.

"The fighters come screaming across the desert in the night, yelling Arabic curses as they fire their guns," said Abdullah. "We don't have night vision goggles, so we shoot at the muzzle flashes and hope we hit them. But I never empty my rifle's magazine, because I know what will happen if they capture me. So, I always leave the last bullet for myself.

"Last week, on two nights in a row when we returned to camp, I dreamed that a man glowing with brilliant white light saved my life. I don't believe in God, but I am troubled. Perhaps you can help me."

The young soldier's face flinched when we asked him to elaborate. It was obvious that, having left the storm of battle, a different tempest was raging in his soul.

On the day after his second dream, Abdullah said, his squad had chased ISIS out of a village and was searching house to house for rigged explosives.

"My commander told me to check a certain house," he said, "but when I reached for the doorknob I felt that glowing presence beside me, as if it were touching my arm and warning me to leave. So, I pulled back my hand and walked away. That afternoon, two other soldiers tried to enter that same house and it blew up and killed them.

"What is this presence that saved my life?" asked Abdullah. "Why is this happening to me?"

"Are there some Christians who have been praying for you?" Terry Law asked the soldier.

Abdullah nodded. "Yes, my sister prays for me. We were raised Muslim but she has been following Jesus for five years."

"God obviously listens to your sister's prayers," responded Terry, "and he sent a messenger to warn you."

"You may not believe in God, Abdullah, but obviously he believes in you," added James.

After saying a prayer with Abdullah, we parted ways and the next day left Erbil to return to America. One week later, a car bomb exploded in front of the U.S. Embassy in Erbil, not more than 30 seconds after Abdullah had driven past. At once the young soldier sprang into action and was able to save the life of a wounded American. The next day we received a one-sentence message from him.

"I have decided. I am now a follower of Jesus."

Abdullah had found what ISIS can never take away: peace in midst of the storm. But he is not the only one.

In February 2015, the world looked on in horror when 21 Egyptian workers, all Coptic Christians, were marched to a Libyan seashore and beheaded by ISIS. Especially shaken were the people of Egypt, not only by the grisly event itself but even more by the responses of the victim's families when they were interviewed by Egyptian media. "This only makes us stronger in our faith because the Bible told us to love our enemies and bless those who curse us," said Beshir Kamel, whose two brothers were among the martyrs. "God forgives the sinners, so shall we," said the daughter of another victim.

What U.N. declaration has ever brought such peace? What army can command it?

We have written previously about our interview with the Syriac Orthodox Archbishop of Mosul, His Eminence Mor Nicodemus Daoud Sharaf. Knowing that the Archbishop had fled his church at the last moment, with ISIS less than a quarter mile away, we asked him to describe the 2014 invasion of Mosul.

Half a million people had fled the city in a panic, he said, heading either 40 miles northward to the city of Duhok or to Erbil, some 50 miles to the east. ISIS checkpoints at the edges of the city ensured that they took nothing with them save the clothes on their backs. Daytime temperatures reached as high as 125 degrees Fahrenheit, with infants and the elderly among the first to succumb during the long, hellish walk to safety. Altogether, the exodus included approximately 160,000 Christians, some 10,000 of them from the Archbishop's diocese.

Did people have the choice to stay and pay *jizya*, the heavy tax imposed on non-believers for the privilege of living in a Muslim society? No, said the Archbishop. They were given 48 hours to leave the city with nothing, to pray the *Shahada* ("Allah is one God and Muhammad is his prophet") or to die.

"How many of your people recanted their Christianity in order to keep their homes?" we asked.

The Archbishop responded with a puzzled look at first, and then answered.

"Perhaps five or six mentally disabled people remained," he said, "and several hundred were beheaded because they stayed but refused to deny the name of Jesus. Everyone else left. They can take our belongings, you see, but they cannot take God from our hearts."

The Archbishop's voice began to break.

"Now, in three days we will celebrate the resurrection of our Lord," he said, his ruddy face turning nearly crimson. "It is the first Easter since Apostle Thomas brought us the gospel on his way to India 2,000 years ago that we cannot celebrate in Mosul. Now there are no Christians left, and our church building has become a mosque."

The interview paused while the Archbishop wept into a tissue and attempted to compose himself.

"We are your elder brothers in Christ," he continued after a few moments. "We still speak Aramaic, because it was the language of Jesus when the gospel came to us. We are your family and we are suffering.

St. Paul said, 'if one member of the body suffers, the whole body suffers.' You are a kind people; please do not forget us."

His Eminence stopped for a moment and lowered his eyes, clearly weighing his next words.

"A friend of mine moved to Australia to build homes," he began in a thoughtful tone. "He was about to develop a large project when heavy rains came, and a few days later eight rare frogs were discovered in a small pond that had formed. 'Monte,' he told me, 'I had to spend one million Australian dollars to build a new habitat for those frogs.'"

The Archbishop's eyes flashed and he raised his palms high above his shoulders.

"A million dollars to build a place for eight frogs and my people are here with nothing! We have lost our place and are forgotten; we have no more dignity. Please...only treat us like those frogs and we will be happy!"

There was little left to say as we bade farewell to Archbishop Daoud and climbed into our bodyguard's SUV on that sunny afternoon. Inwardly, we were both convicted and conflicted. Journalistic integrity normally requires letting the facts in a story stand on their own, free of advocacy and agenda. But one call from family changes everything. In this case, our suffering elder brothers and sisters had begged us not to forget them, and we had promised their bishop that we would tell their story to the world.

The problem is, there is so much to tell. Today less than 250,000 Christians remain in Iraq, compared to more than 1.5 million as recently as 2003. This is because, aside from displacing Christians (and other minorities), ISIS has slaughtered untold thousands more. It is a horror that has prompted a host of voices, including Speaker of the House of Representatives Paul Ryan, hundreds of House members,

Pope Francis, and Democrat Presidential candidate Hillary Clinton, to call for an official declaration of genocide.

Beyond Iraq, the refugee situation is constantly fluid, as wave after wave of humanity washes up against the borders of various European countries reluctant to take them in. But what can they do? No civilized people wants to see a little boy's body floating face down in the surf, but neither can they tolerate the rash of assaults and rapes at the hands of immigrants in countries like France and Sweden. In the U.S., Congress and the White House struggle with our nation's own admittance policies, caught between calls for compassion and vows to build a wall. Thus, both the debate and the storm rage on.

As for what can be done, we have already recommended several steps that you can take, not only in calling for decisive action on the part of America's leaders, but also to protect yourself, your family and friends from attacks on the homeland. But there is more. In fact, your greatest power lies in taking two final steps.

In publishing this book, *The Storm Chaser Foundation* has taken you into the eye of the terrorist storm, not only to educate you about ISIS, but also to equip you to help bring peace and safety to those battered by it. Remember, Jesus was not standing on the shore when he calmed the storm; he was in its midst, right there in the boat with those whose lives were in danger.

Unmasking ISIS is your invitation to become a Storm Chaser, to step into the boat and make a difference. Here's how.

First, you can pray. Prayer is often the last resort of a rebellious people who waited too long to put it first. Even amongst self-professing Christians, it is frequently cordoned off for meals and bedtimes, if not abandoned altogether. Our old friend, a legendary Bible smuggler known as Brother Andrew, captures the problem.

> Some time ago I heard two Christian women discussing the plight of hostages being held by Middle Eastern terrorists.
>
> "I feel sorry for those poor men and their families," one of the women remarked, "but really this is God's problem, not ours. We have to remember that he has already decided how their stories are going to turn out."
>
> The other woman sighed. "Yes," she said, "but it's frustrating! It seems we are all being held hostage by the evil people in the world—the terrorists, and dictators, the drug dealers, the criminals...."
>
> The first woman smiled and patted her friend's arm. "Well, that's how it looks," she said comfortingly. "But we know God has His reasons for allowing these things. Even when we don't understand those reasons, we can be sure nothing happens outside his will.
>
> As I listened I felt indignation rising inside me. I could barely control the urge to turn to them and say, "What's the matter with you? Why are you talking this way? You are not helpless! God has given you the power to change that situation! Why don't you use it? Why don't you pray?"[125]

As a missionary renowned for smuggling significant aid to persecuted Christians, often right under the noses of dictators and their henchmen, Andrew burns with indignation at what he calls the "doctrine of Christian fatalism." that, in these women's case, "neutralized their effectiveness as believers....[T]he truth is, their beliefs about 'God's will' would have fit very nicely into the Muslim religion, and into a number of other fatalistic religions, too.'"[126]

Please do not set this book aside or place it back in your library. Instead, set it on your nightstand, coffee table or mantle—wherever you and your family spend your time. Let it be your reminder to pray, not once but every day, for the refugee families huddled in caves and culverts, the tortured farmers of Raqqa, Syria, the mothers in Toronto or Toulouse whose sons have disappeared, the panicked French girl who wishes she could escape the hell she thought would be paradise, and for the widows and orphans. There are so many widows and orphans.

Second, in addition to prayer, you can act. Remember German martyr Dietrich Bonhoeffer's words: "Silence in the face of evil is itself evil. God will not hold us guiltless. Not to speak is to speak. Not to act is to act."

Following is a list of six effective, efficient non-governmental organizations of proven integrity, who are working tirelessly to help Christians and other refugees in the Middle East. Please go to their websites, call or write, and see for yourself what they are doing and how you can participate.

World Compassion (www.worldcompassion.tv)
PO Box 92
Tulsa OK 74101

Samaritan's Purse (www.samaritanspurse.org)
P.O. Box 3000
Boone, NC 28607

World Help (www.worldhelp.net/Iraq)
PO Box 501
Forest VA 24551

The Cradle Fund (www.cradlefund.org)
PO Box 12205
Arlington VA 22219

Knights of Columbus (http://ChristiansAtRisk.org/)
1 Columbus Plaza
New Haven, CT 06510

Voice of the Martyrs (www.persecution.com)
PO Box 443
Bartlesville OK 74005

NOTES

1. Quoted by Episcopal News Service, August 8, 2104, accessed on May 30, 2015, http://episcopaldigitalnetwork.com/ens/2014/08/08/anglican-vicar-of-baghdad-child-i-baptized-cut-in-half-by-isis/

2. Interview with Orthodox Christian Network, quoted at DailyMail.com, December 12, 2014, accessed on May 30, 2015, http://www.dailymail.co.uk/news/article-2871508/Four-young-Christians-brutally-beheaded-ISIS-Iraq-refusing-convert-Islam-says-Vicar-Baghdad-Canon-Andrew-White.html

3. Gilbert, James. Storm Chaser: The Terry Law Story. Tulsa: Storm Chaser Media, 2014

4. HOW MANY FIGHTERS DOES THE ISLAMIC STATE REALLY HAVE, February 9, 2015, accessed on June 16, 2015 at http://warontherocks.com/2015/02/how-many-fighters-does-the-islamic-state-really-have/?singlepage=1

5. War with Isis: Islamic militants have army of 200,000, claims senior Kurdish leader. The Independent UK, November 16, 2014, accessed on June 16, 2015 at http://www.independent.co.uk/news/world/middle-east/war-with-isis-islamic-militants-have-army-of-200000-claims-kurdish-leader-9863418.html

6. Accessed on June 12, 2015 at http://www.thedailybeast.com/articles/2014/06/14/isis-leader-see-you-in-new-york.html

7. Accessed on June 16, 2015 at https://en.wikipedia.org/wiki/Constitution_of_Medina.

8. Modern Islam teaches that Muhammad was poisoned by Jews.

9. Armstrong, Karen (2007-12-18). Islam: A Short History (Modern Library Chronicles Series Book 2) (Kindle Locations 75-86). Random House Publishing Group. Kindle Edition.

10. The Federalist Papers Project, accessed on February 22, 2016 at http://www.thefederalistpapers.org/founders/thomas-jefferson-quotes

11. Armstrong, Karen (2013-08-13), Muhammad: A Prophet for Our Time (Kindle Locations 98-99). HarperCollins. Kindle Edition.

12. See Army of the Men of the Naqshbandi Order, accessed on July 3, 2015 at https://en.wikipedia.org/wiki/Army_of_the_Men_of_the_Naqshbandi_Order, for a description of a Sufist militant group that has purportedly joined itself to ISIS.

13. From the Hadith, Sahih al-Bukhari • Oaths and Vows, Narrated Zahdam bin Mudarrab, accessed on July 5, 2015 at http://sunnah.com/search/?q=my+generation.

14. Khan, Maulana Wahiduddin; Goodword (2013-12-11). Qur'an: A Simple English Translation (Goodword! Koran) (Kindle Location 1626). Goodword Books. Kindle Edition.

15. http://dictionary.reference.com/browse/qiyas

16. Top intel official confirms ISIS made, used chemical weapons. February 9, 2105, accessed on February 15, 2016 at http://www.foxnews.com/politics/2016/02/09/top-intel-official-confirms-isis-made-used-chemical-weapons.html?intcmp=hpbt2

17. See "List of groups designated terrorist organisations by the UAE," accessed on, July 7, 2015, at http://www.thenational.ae/uae/government/list-of-groups-designated-terrorist-organisations-by-the-uae.

18. http://www.businessinsider.com/al-qaeda-application-2015-5, accessed on, July 8, 2015.

19. World Politics Review, Wednesday, September 11, 2013, "Jihad 2020: Assessing Al-Qaida's 20-Year Plan" by Aaron Y. Zelin, accessed on October 13, 2015 at http://www.worldpoliticsreview.com/articles/13208/jihad-2020-assessing-al-qaida-s-20-year-plan

20. Vol. 5, Book 36, Hadith 4084, accessed on August 31. 2015 at http://sunnah.com/ibnmajah/36/159

21. Ramadan is an annual month-long fast that commemorates Muhammad's revelation of the Qur'an.

22. Quoted in Lawrence, James, The Golden Warrior: The life nd legend of Lawrence of Arabia. p. 129. New York: Skyhorse Publishing, 2008.

23. Ibid.

24. https://en.wikipedia.org/wiki/Balfour_Declaration, accessed on July 9, 2015.

25. Afzal Ashraf, The myth of the caliphate and the Islamic State, Al Jazeera, July 10, 2014, accessed on February 22, 2016 at http://www.aljazeera.com/indepth/opinion/2014/07/myth-caliphate-islamic-state-20147912425476113.html.

26. From OPINION: ISIS Appeals to a Longing for the caliphate, Inter Press News Service, September 24, 2014, accessed on August 12, 2015 at http://www.ipsnews.net/2014/09/opinion-isis-appeals-to-a-longing-for-the-caliphate/.

27. What ISIS Really Wants, by Graeme Wood, The Atlantic, March 2015 Issue, accessed on August 14, 2015 at http://www.theatlantic.com/features/archive/2015/02/what-isis-really-wants/384980/

28. Ibid.

29. Al-Baghdadi's sermon: "This is the Promise of Allah," June 29, 2014, accessed on August 14, 2015 at https://ia902505.us.archive.org/28/items/poa_25984/EN.pdf

30. Ibid.

31. Of much greater historical significance, the 1979 Iranian Revolution, and the declaration of the Islamic Republic of Iran by Ayatollah Ruhollah Khomeini, brought an end not only to the house of Pahlavi, but also to more than 4,600 years of Iranian monarchy itself.

32. Jahanpour, OPINION: ISIS Appeals to a Longing for the caliphate

33. Isis are barbarians—but the caliphate is an ancient Muslim ideal, by John Casey, The Independent, July 4, 2015, accessed on August 17, 2015 at http://www.independent.co.uk/voices/comment/isis-are-barbarians--but-the-caliphate-is-an-ancient-muslim-ideal-10365201.html

34. Hall, Benjamin (2015-03-10). Inside ISIS: The Brutal Rise of a Terrorist Army (pp. 14-15). Center Street. Kindle Edition.

35. Nearly a year later, in April 2015, the Iraqi army claimed to have killed al-Douri in Tikrit, but an audio recording purporting to be his voice was released a month later specifically to refute the claim.

36. Ibid. p. 16.

37. Erelle, Anna; Potter, Erin (2015-05-26). In the Skin of a Jihadist: A Young Journalist Enters the ISIS Recruitment Network (pp. 3-4). HarperCollins. Kindle Edition.

38. Pseudonym

39. "Mothers of ISIS," by Julia Joffe, August 12, 2015, accessed on September 8, 2015 at http://highline.huffingtonpost.com/articles/en/mothers-of-isis/

40. Interview with Public Radio International, January 13, 2015, accessed on August 20. 2015 at http://www.pri.org/stories/2015-01-13/christianne-boudreau-lost-her-son-when-he-went-fight-isis-now-shes-doing

41. "How ISIS's $2B budget helps it recruit Western teenagers to terrorism," March 27, 2015, accessed on September 2, 2015 at http://www.cnn.com/2015/03/27/opinions/aamer-isis-recruiting-western-teenagers/.

42. Ibid.

43. "ISIS and the Lonely Young American," June 27, 2015, accessed on September 3, 2015 at http://www.nytimes.com/2015/06/28/world/americas/isis-on-recruiting-american.html?_r=0

44. Quoted in "From Scottish teen to ISIS bride and recruiter: the Aqsa Mahmood story," accessed September 2, 2015 at http://www.cnn.com/2015/02/23/world/scottish-teen-isis-recruiter/index.html

45. Erelle, Anna; Potter, Erin (2015-05-26). In the Skin of a Jihadist: A Young Journalist Enters the ISIS Recruitment Network (p. 3). HarperCollins. Kindle Edition.

46. http://www.mirror.co.uk/news/uk-news/reality-life-isis-bride-former-6085180, accessed on September 4, 2015

47. "The Calgary mother fighting radicalisation in Syria," accessed on September 4, 2015 at http://www.bbc.com/news/magazine-32539638

48. Loc.cit. "Mothers of ISIS."

49. "ISIS Enshrines a Theology of Rape," August 13, 2015, accessed on September 8, 2015 at http://www.nytimes.com/2015/08/14/world/middleeast/isis-enshrines-a-theology-of-rape.html?_r=0.

50. English translation accessed on at: http://www.noblequran.com/translation/

51. Accessed on at: http://sunnah.com/abudawud/12

52. Bush, George W. (2010-11-09). Decision Points (p. 194). Random House, Inc.. Kindle Edition.

53. Transparency International's Corruption Perception Index 2014, accessed on October 12, 2015 at http://www.transparency.org/cpi2014/results

54. Woodward, Bob: Plan of Attack: The Definitive Account of the Decision to Invade Iraq (New York: Simon & Schuster, Inc., 2004) P. 150.

55. The Pottery Barn Rule: Syria Edition, September 30, 2015, by Kathy Gilsinan, accessed on October 8, 2015 at http://www.theatlantic.com/international/archive/2015/09/the-pottery-barn-rule-syria-edition/408193/

56. Bush, George W. (2010-11-09). Decision Points (pp. 248-249). Random House, Inc.. Kindle Edition.

57. Dabiq Magazine, Issue 7, p. 20.

58. Ali, Ayaan Hirsi (2015-03-24). Heretic: Why Islam Needs a Reformation Now (p. 24). HarperCollins. Kindle Edition.

59. Remarks by the President to the White House Press Corps, August 20, 2012, accessed on October 13, 2013 at https://www.whitehouse.gov/the-press-office/2012/08/20/remarks-president-white-house-press-corps

60. U.S. Shoots Itself in the Foot by Accidentally Arming ISIS, by Eric Pianin, June 4, 2015, accessed on October 22, 2015 at http://www.thefiscaltimes.com/2015/06/04/Fog-War-US-Has-Armed-ISIS

61. DailyMail.com, Isis profits from destruction of antiquities by selling relics to dealers – and then blowing up the buildings they come from to conceal the evidence of looting. June 11, 2015, accessed on October 21, 2015 at http://www.independent.co.uk/voices/isis-profits-from-destruction-of-antiquities-by-selling-relics-to-dealers-and-then-blowing-up-the-10483421.html

62. CBSnews.com, Following the trail of Syria's looted history, September 9, 2015, accessed on October 22, 2015 at http://www.cbsnews.com/news/isis-looted-syrian-ancient-artifacts-black-market-us-and-europe/

63. FoxNews.com, July 24, 2015, accessed on October 22, 2015 at http://www.foxnews.com/politics/2015/07/24/isis-gained-up-to-1b-in-cash-after-taking-over-mosul-official-says/?cmpid=cmty_twitter_fn#

64. How Does ISIS Fund its Reign of Terror?, Newsweek, November 6, 2014, accessed on October 24, 2015 at http://www.newsweek.com/2014/11/14/how-does-isis-fund-its-reign-terror-282607.html

65. Islamic State Makes Millions in Ransom, Expert Says, November 25, 2014, accessed on October 24, 2015 at http://unitedwithisrael.org/islamic-state-makes-millions-in-ransom-expert-says/

66. NYDailyNews.com, August 21, 2014, accessed on October 24, 2015 at http://www.nydailynews.com/news/world/isis-demanded-132m-ransom-killing-james-foley-article-1.1911515http://www.nydailynews.com/news/world/isis-demanded-132m-ransom-killing-james-foley-article-1.1911515

67. Idem., Newsweek, November 6, 2014

68. NYTimes.com, Paying Ransoms, Europe Bankrolls Qaeda Terror, July 29, 2014, accessed on October 24, 2015 at http://www.nytimes.com/2014/07/30/world/africa/ransoming-citizens-europe-becomes-al-qaedas-patron.html?_r=0

69. Ibid.

70. Idem., Newsweek, November 6, 2014

71. BloombergBusiness, Islamic State Circulates Sex Slave Price List, August 3, 2015, accessed on October 24, 2015 at http://www.bloomberg.com/news/articles/2015-08-03/sex-slaves-sold-by-islamic-state-the-younger-the-better

72. Accessed on October 26, 2015 at http://jihadology.net/2015/10/05/the-archivist-unseen-islamic-state-financial-accounts-for-deir-az-zor-province/

73. Hall, Benjamin (2015-03-10). Inside ISIS: The Brutal Rise of a Terrorist Army (p. 162). Center Street. Kindle Edition.

74. Accessed on October 26, 2015 at http://english.alarabiya.net/en/News/middle-east/2015/09/07/ISIS-takes-Syrian-state-s-last-oilfield-.html

75. Accessed on October 26, 2015 at http://www.breitbart.com/national-security/2015/08/21/report-isis-mafias-earned-11-million-in-iraq-through-extortion/

76. The ISIS Economy: Crushing Taxes and High Unemployment , September 2, 2015, accessed on October 26, 2015 at http://www.theatlantic.com/international/archive/2015/09/isis-territory-taxes-recruitment-syria/403426/

77. Idem.

78. Idem., Newsweek, November 6, 2014

79. TIME Magazine, November 30, 2015, How to Beat ISIS, pp. 49-57.

80. Obama Must Lead the World's Efforts to Defeat the Islamic State, by Stewart M. Patrick, NEWSWEEK.com, November 19, 2015, accessed on November 21, 2015 at http://www.newsweek.com/obama-must-lead-worlds-efforts-defeat-isis-396299

81. Andrea Mitchell Reports, November 16, 2015, accessed on November 21, 2015 at http://www.msnbc.com/andrea-mitchell-reports/watch/feinstein---i-ve-never-been-more-concerned--567674435736.

82. Brookings.edu, After the Spring: Inclusive Growth in the Arab World, January 30, 2013, accessed on November 20, 2015 at http://www.brookings.edu/blogs/up-front/posts/2013/01/30-inclusive-growth-arab-world-ghanem

83. TIME Cover story, Nov 30/Dec 7, 2015

84. Name withheld by request.

85. Daily Mail, December 9, 2015, accessed on February 9, 2016 at http://www.dailymail.co.uk/news/article-3352494/Has-ISIS-leader-escaped-Libya-Sources-claim-Al-Baghdadi-fled-Gaddafi-s-hometown-Sirte.html

86. Weiss, Michael; Hassan, Hassan (2015-01-29). ISIS: Inside the Army of Terror (pp. 123-124). Regan Arts. Kindle Edition.

87. Accessed on December 4, 2015 at https://www.judicialwatch.org/wp-content/uploads/2015/05/Pg.-291-Pgs.-287-293-JW-v-DOD-and-State-14-812-DOD-Release-2015-04-10-final-version11.pdf.

88. Accessed on December 11, 2015 at http://www.cnn.com/2012/08/01/us/syria-rebels-us-aid/

89. Accessed on December 11, 2015 at http://www.washingtontimes.com/news/2012/aug/2/obama-arming-al-qaeda/

90. Interview with Megyn Kelly, "The Kelly File," FNC, November 23, 2015, accessed on December 4, 2015 at http://www.foxnews.com/politics/2015/11/23/former-head-defense-intelligence-agency-responds-to-claims-over-isis-intelligence.html.

91. Interview with Jake Tapper, "The Lead," CNN, December 2, 2015, accessed on December 4, 2015 at http://www.cnn.com/2015/12/01/politics/michael-flynn-obama-isis/.

92. Accessed on December 1, 2015, at http://www.al-bab.com/arab/docs/pal/pal10.htm

93. Lawrence, Quil (2009-05-26). Invisible Nation: How the Kurds' Quest for Statehood Is Shaping Iraq and the Middle East (p. 4). Bloomsbury Publishing. Kindle Edition.

94. Ibid, pp. 4-5.

95. Accessed at http://www.liquisearch.com/israeli–kurdish_relations/political_relations on December 2, 2015

96. Wall Street Journal, December 4, 2015, On the Front Line Against Islamic State, accessed on December 4, 2015 at http://www.wsj.com/articles/on-the-front-line-against-islamic-state-1449273142

97. See http://www.thedailybeast.com/articles/2015/12/06/us-intel-to-obama-isis-is-not-contained.html

98. Huffington Post, July 1, 2015, accessed on December 7, 2015 at http://www.huffingtonpost.com/2015/06/29/congress-arm-kurds_n_7647068.html.

99. New York Times, To Save Iraq, Arm the Kurds, by Aliza Marcus and Andrew Apostolou, accessed on December 7, 2015 at http://www.nytimes.com/2015/10/12/opinion/to-save-iraq-arm-the-kurds.html?_r=0

100. Mansfield, Stephen (2014-10-14). The Miracle of the Kurds: A Remarkable Story of Hope Reborn In Northern Iraq (p. 82). Worthy Publishing. Kindle Edition

101. For more information, see http://www.museumoflondon.org.uk/explore-on/pocket-histories/what-was-life-london-during-world-war-ii/community-spirit/

102. Accessed on January 29, 2016 at https://www.numbersusa.com/news/dhs-nearly-500000-foreign-visitors-overstayed-their-visa-2015

103. Accessed on January 29, 2016 at https://www.numbersusa.com/news/report-dhs-lost-track-thousands-foreign-students-"heightened-concern"

104. See http://www.immigration-professor.com/obama-signs-omnibus-spending-bill-into-law-raises-h1b-visa-fee-01442.htm

105. Accessed on December 16, 2015 at http://www.foxnews.com/us/2015/12/16/as-lawmakers-clash-over-refugees-syrian-immigration-quietly-tops-100000-since/?intcmp=hpbt1

106. See http://www.bbc.com/news/world-middle-east-33690060

107. See http://www.nationalreview.com/article/427619/state-department-iran-deal-not-legally-binding-signed.

108. Accessed on December 17, 2015 at http://english.alarabiya.net/en/News/middle-east/2015/12/17/Tunisian-Nobel-winners-marking-5-years-of-Arab-Spring.html. The remark, by a senior advisor to the Iranian President, was quickly walked back within days. Unofficially, however, the notion persists.

109. http://www.nbcnews.com/tech/security/isis-has-app-could-they-build-encryption-tools-too-n471596

110. http://www.huffingtonpost.com/entry/anonymous-isis_5649610ae4b045bf3defc173

111. Dara, Khurram (2015-12-01). Contracting Fear: Islamic Law in the Middle East and Middle America. Cascade Books, an Imprint of Wipf and Stock Publishers. Kindle Edition.

112. http://cslr.law.emory.edu/people/person/name/ahmed-an-naim/

113. Ali, Ayaan Hirsi (2015-03-24). Heretic: Why Islam Needs a Reformation Now. HarperCollins. Kindle Edition.

114. Accessed on 1/24/16 at https://www.youtube.com/watch?v=afjAeXVaezs

115. Ali, Ayaan Hirsi (2015-03-24). Heretic: Why Islam Needs a Reformation Now (p. 2). HarperCollins. Kindle Edition.

116. http://www.michaelyon.com

117. http://www.nicoletung.com

118. Accessed on December 16, 2015 at http://www.raabcollection.com/harry-truman-autograph/harry-truman-writes-purpose-press#sthash.3wDrvfMT.dpuf.

119. See, for example, http://www.fredericksburg.com/news/local/christians-muslims-team-up-in-fredericksburg-area-to-help-refugees/article_6488c7cb-fb26-5439-bc3f-85de1d207f67.html

120. Quoted at http://groups.colgate.edu/aarislam/susan.htm, accessed on January 30, 2106.

121. Accessed on January 30, 2016 at http://www.thenation.com/article/blowback/

122. The PEW Research Center reported in 2015 that at least a quarter of young adults aged 18-34 still lived in their parents' homes. See http://www.pewsocialtrends.org/2015/07/29/more-millennials-living-with-family-despite-improved-job-market/

123. See https://www.commonsensemedia.org/about-us/our-mission#

124. Accessed on January 25, 2016 at http://www.jihadwatch.org/2015/12/sb-area-man-didnt-report-suspicious-activity-for-fear-of-being-called-racist

125. Andrew, Brother, with Susan DeVore Williams, And God Changed His Mind (Grand Rapids: Chosen Books., 1999), pp. 11, 12.

126. Ibid., p. 12.

ACKNOWLEDGMENTS

The authors wish to thank Mr. and Mrs. George and Linda Wiland, and Mr. and Mrs. Dean and Carol Ann Eldridge, for their steadfast support from the beginning of this endeavor.

Our deepest gratitude also to the Honorable Karim Sinjari, Minister of the Interior, Kurdistan Region, Iraq, Major General Aziz Waisi, Commander of Kurdistan's Peshmerga Zerevani Force, members of the Peshmerga Christian brigade, His Eminence Mor Nicodemus Daoud, Archbishop of Mosul, General Georges Sada, and Mr. Nabil Omeish of the United Bible Society for their valuable assistance during our time in the Kurdistan Region of Iraq.

Dr. Chris van Gorder, Associate Professor of World Religions & Islamic Studies at Baylor University, and Dr. David S. Oualaalou, International Security Lecturer, were of great help in keeping us on course amid the turbulent waters and countless tributaries of Middle Eastern history.

Thanks also to Dr. Daniel Gilbert, Dr. J.R. Tayler, Sherri Ward and Alan Sargent for making sure we said everything in English, and to David Hazard of ASCENT, who manages to take our best and make it better.

Special thanks to Chris Thompson, for asking the right question at the right moment.

Finally, thank you to our wives and children for your unwavering love and support. The journey into darkness is made easier when one is anchored by the light from home.

ABOUT THE AUTHORS

DR. TERRY LAW is president of The Storm Chaser Foundation and founder of World Compassion, a humanitarian aid ministry headquartered in Tulsa, Oklahoma. For decades he has supplied life-saving relief to persecuted peoples in dozens of nations, including Iraq, Afghanistan, Russia and China. He consults with government and religious leaders internationally, with a special focus on the Middle East and the Muslim world. The author of several books, he is a widely-sought speaker in the United States, Canada and Europe. He and his wife, Barbara live in Tulsa, Oklahoma.

JAMES GILBERT is co-founder of The Storm Chaser Foundation. His wide-ranging career as an author, speaker and recording artist has taken him into 61 nations on five continents, with special emphasis on the Middle East, Cuba and Eastern Europe. A versatile communicator, he has lectured in Moscow's City Hall, performed at a Soviet jazz festival, conducted medical clinics in China, interviewed Iraqi government leaders and taught philosophy in an American high school. He is the author of six books, including *Storm Chaser: The Terry Law Story*. James lives with his wife and daughter in Florida.

MAKE A DIFFERENCE CHANGE YOUR WORLD

Just as *Unmasking ISIS* informed you about terror in the Middle East, *Storm Chaser: The Terry Law Story* captures the remarkable life of a daredevil minister whose 50 year career in Christian missions and humanitarian work has taken him from Soviet KGB interrogations to Moscow's evening news, and from Vatican concerts with Pope John Paul II to secret diplomatic missions in Iraq.

More than a riveting adventure, *Storm Chaser* includes key principles to help readers go beyond surviving life's storms and discover that "in the eye of every storm lies the power of God to change your world."

ORDER STORM CHASER IN PAPERBACK OR KINDLE E-BOOK FROM AMAZON.COM

www.StormChaser.org